Retail 4.0

How AI is Shaping
the Future of Shopping

By
Julia Carrington

Retail 4.0

How AI is Shaping
the Future of Shopping

Table of Contents

Introduction

In the bustling world of retail, change is a constant companion. It's driven by the relentless march of technological innovation, with Artificial Intelligence (AI) playing a pivotal role in the current transformation. Once a mere concept in the realm of science fiction, AI has rapidly leaped into the very core of modern commerce, redefining how businesses operate and how customers engage with them. This book aims to delve into this phenomenal shift, offering a comprehensive exploration of AI's profound impact on the retail landscape.

We stand at a crossroads where AI is not merely augmenting existing systems but fundamentally reshaping the entire retail ecosystem. Retailers are beginning to experience a paradigm shift: from personalized shopping experiences that cater to individual preferences to dynamic pricing strategies that anticipate market fluctuations with uncanny accuracy. These advances, empowered by AI, pave the way for a new era of retail intelligence, where every decision is informed by data and driven by insights.

The fusion of AI and retail holds unparalleled potential for innovation. Today, forward-thinking professionals and entrepreneurs are keenly interested in understanding and harnessing this potential. They recognize that AI technologies offer more than just operational efficiency; they represent a strategic advantage in an increasingly competitive marketplace. As the retail world becomes more interconnected, those who can strategically leverage AI will find themselves at the forefront of industry evolution.

To appreciate the full scope of AI's impact, we must first understand the context in which it operates. The traditional retail model, which once relied heavily on intuition and trend forecasting, is evolving into an agile, data-driven organism. The use of AI in retail is unraveling new possibilities: streamlining supply chain operations, refining inventory management, and creating personalized customer experiences that were once beyond imagination.

AI's entry into the retail sector is not just about technology; it's about a transformation in thinking. Retailers are now envisioning a future where innovation leads to enhanced customer satisfaction and business growth. By combining AI's analytical power with human creativity, businesses can unlock new avenues for engagement, creating shopping experiences that are not only efficient but also enriched with intuitive human touch.

In this book, you will encounter the multifaceted role AI plays at various junctions in the retail landscape. Chapters will cover key topics like personalized shopping, supply chain optimization, customer service automation, and much more. Each chapter sheds light on the challenges and opportunities AI presents, offering actionable insights to help you harness these cutting-edge technologies for maximum impact.

Importantly, we must also acknowledge the ethical and societal implications of widespread AI adoption. As AI becomes more integrated into retail operations, questions around data privacy, consumer trust, and job displacement arise. Addressing these challenges is crucial for building a sustainable and equitable retail environment that benefits everyone.

Understanding AI's current capabilities and potential future is essential for any retail professional aiming for long-term success. As AI technology continues to evolve rapidly, so too will the retail sector, prompting businesses to adapt and innovate continuously. By embracing AI, companies can not only streamline operations but also position themselves for future growth in a world where digital and physical retail environments are inseparably linked.

This introduction sets the stage for an insightful journey through the transformative role of AI in retail. Our exploration will illuminate how embracing AI doesn't just mean adopting new technologies but fostering a culture of innovation that thrives on harnessing the power of data and technology. With AI, the future of retail is not just about meeting customer needs—it's about anticipating them.

Through the pages that follow, readers will gain a deeper understanding of how AI is molding the future of commerce. Whether you're a seasoned professional, a curious entrepreneur, or a dedicated tech enthusiast, this book will equip you with the knowledge and foresight to navigate the exciting frontier of AI in retail. Welcome to a world where the possibilities are as boundless as our imagination.

Chapter 1:
The Rise of AI in Retail

The retail industry is witnessing a transformative revolution, driven by the explosive integration of artificial intelligence (AI) that is reshaping how businesses operate and engage with consumers. This chapter delves into the emergence of AI as a pivotal force in retail, examining how it is spurring profound changes in consumer behavior and catalyzing a shift towards more efficient retail operations. With machine learning algorithms dissecting vast amounts of data, retailers are now equipped to anticipate customer needs with unparalleled precision, enhancing both the shopper's experience and the retailer's efficiency. The dawn of AI technology in retail signifies not just incremental improvements but a paradigm shift, offering a chance to reimagine and redesign the entirety of the retail landscape. As retailers begin to harness AI's full potential, they are transforming storefronts and online spaces into smarter, more adaptive environments that promise to redefine the future of commerce. This evolution presents opportunities for retailers to innovate, creating resilient strategies that are both adaptable and customer-centric in an increasingly competitive market.

Impact on Consumer Behavior

The retail landscape is undergoing a seismic shift as Artificial Intelligence becomes more ingrained in the shopping experience. For consumers, this isn't just about convenience or personalization—it's a profound change in behavior and expectations. In recent years, AI has introduced technologies that redefine how shoppers interact with brands and make purchasing decisions, steering consumer behavior in new directions.

The integration of AI in retail has increased the prevalence of personalized shopping experiences. AI algorithms analyze past purchase history, browsing patterns, and even social media activity to tailor offers and recommendations to individual preferences. This meticulous customization transforms how consumers view the brands they engage with. Rather than a faceless entity, a brand now appears as a thoughtful, adaptive companion on the consumer's shopping journey.

With the introduction of AI-driven virtual assistants and chatbots, the dynamics of consumer interaction have evolved significantly. These automated entities are not only available 24/7 but are also becoming adept at understanding complex queries and providing quick responses. This level of accessibility fosters a sense of immediacy and satisfaction, encouraging consumers to make shopping decisions swiftly and with increased confidence. Consumers now expect interactions to be seamless and available around the clock.

AI's analytic capabilities enable retailers to predict trends and respond with agility—before consumers even realize a demand exists. This predictive power significantly affects purchasing behaviors by introducing consumers to products they might not have considered otherwise. As a result, consumers find themselves exploring a broader range of products and making unplanned purchases, driven by data-informed suggestions they trust and value.

Moreover, AI's impact extends beyond influencing purchases in the digital realm; it also plays a significant role in the physical retail environment. In-store technologies such as smart mirrors and AI-enhanced RFID (Radio Frequency Identification) sensors provide consumers with instant information and feedback. These interactive elements dissolve the line between online and offline shopping, creating a holistic experience that satisfies the evolving expectations of today's tech-savvy consumer.

As AI continues to redefine retail, consumers are becoming more data-literate and aware of their digital footprints. The trade-off for personalized experiences often involves sharing personal data, prompting consumers to weigh convenience against privacy. This awareness is reshaping consumer attitudes toward data sharing, now seen not just as a transactional choice but as a significant aspect of brand loyalty and trust. Retailers must navigate these waters carefully, as consumer behavior is becoming increasingly tied to ethical considerations around data use.

The rise of AI in retail further amplifies the effectiveness of loyalty programs. By analyzing consumer data, AI enables more dynamic and targeted rewards, fostering deeper brand affinity. This precision nurtures a more engaged consumer base, as shoppers feel their unique preferences are recognized and rewarded in a meaningful way. Consequently, loyalty programs driven by AI show promising trends in retaining customers for longer periods, altering how loyalty is cultivated and measured.

In addition, artificial intelligence is driving a cultural shift towards more informed and empowered consumers. With greater access to information facilitated by AI-powered tools, shoppers are making more calculated decisions. They thoroughly research, compare, and validate products, honing their decision-making skills in an environment saturated with data. This empowerment leads to an emphasis on quality and relevancy rather than brand-driven marketing alone.

Furthermore, the notion of instant gratification is increasingly normalized as AI sophistication merges with e-commerce. Quick delivery algorithms, AI-driven logistics, and real-time inventory assessments ensure that products reach consumers faster than ever before. As consumers grow accustomed to this rapid service, anticipation in decision-making diminishes, prompting retailers to prioritize speed as a key component of customer satisfaction.

AI's transformative power also extends into the sustainability domain, which plays a notably influential role in consumer buying habits. Sustainability-conscious consumers are seeking brands with transparent, eco-friendly practices, often made more visible through AI technologies. By optimizing supply chains and reducing waste, AI not only aids retailers in achieving eco-friendly operations but also attracts consumers who prioritize sustainability in their shopping criteria.

The intersection of AI and retail is more than a mere technological advance; it represents a behavioral evolution. Consumers are not just adopting these changes—they're driving them. As they gravitate toward seamless, personalized experiences, retailers must continue to innovate and adapt. Ultimately, AI's rise in retail is as much about understanding and embracing new consumer paradigms as it is about leveraging cutting-edge technology. Consumers are in command, and those who harness AI effectively will find themselves in a favorable position to meet, or even exceed, the expectations of the modern shopper.

Transforming Retail Operations

The landscape of retail operations is undergoing a seismic shift, driven by the transformative power of artificial intelligence (AI). This transformation is not merely about adopting new technologies; it's about reinventing how retailers operate, manage resources, and engage with customers. By embedding AI into core operational processes, retailers can achieve remarkable efficiencies and improvements in accuracy, speed, and customer satisfaction. As we delve into this section, we'll explore the myriad ways AI is reshaping operational activities, making them leaner, smarter, and more responsive to the ever-changing market dynamics.

One of the most compelling applications of AI in retail operations is its ability to streamline supply chain management. Retailers are using AI-driven tools to enhance visibility across complex supply chains, enabling them to make informed decisions in real-time. This technological integration allows for precise tracking of products from the point of manufacture to the final sale. By anticipating disruptions and recommending optimal shipping routes, AI helps in mitigating risks and reducing costs associated with delays and inefficiencies.

Inventory management, a backbone of retail operations, has witnessed profound changes with AI's integration. AI systems can analyze sales data and consumer trends to predict stock requirements with remarkable accuracy. This foresight prevents the dual hazards of overstocking and stockouts, ensuring that shelves are neither overfilled nor empty. Such precision not only preserves capital but also enhances customer satisfaction by consistently meeting demand.

Furthermore, AI's impact extends to workforce management, where it's revolutionizing how retailers allocate human resources. Predictive analytics helps retailers foresee peak hours of business activity, allowing them to schedule staff efficiently. Employee performance can also be optimized by using AI insights to identify training needs and measure productivity. As AI takes over routine tasks, it empowers employees to focus on customer engagement and strategic activities, driving overall operational excellence.

Operational efficiency is also significantly enhanced by AI's ability to automate repetitive tasks. In areas such as order processing, returns management, and customer service, AI automation is achieving speed and accuracy far beyond human capability. This shift frees up valuable human resources and reduces the likelihood of errors, leading to smoother operations and improved service delivery. AI-driven chatbots, for instance, can handle high volumes of customer inquiries swiftly, leaving complex cases for human intervention.

AI technology is also enabling retailers to optimize product pricing. Dynamic pricing strategies, powered by AI, allow retailers to adjust prices in response to competitor actions, consumer demand, and market conditions. This agility enables retailers to maintain competitive positions and maximize profitability without compromising perceived value. It's an intricate balance of economics and psychology, where AI plays a pivotal role in driving strategic pricing decisions.

Another transformative aspect of AI in retail operations is the enhancement of logistics through predictive analytics. By analyzing patterns and drawing on historical data, AI systems forecast consumer demand and align logistical operations accordingly. This synchronization minimizes wastage, reduces transportation costs, and boosts overall supply chain efficiency.

AI's role in transforming retail operations is profound, but it's not without challenges. Implementing AI solutions requires robust infrastructures, initial investment, and a significant shift in corporate culture. Retailers need to forge a data-driven mindset, embracing AI not just as a tool but as an integral part of their strategic planning. The success of AI in transforming operations hinges on executives' willingness to rethink traditional practices and cultivate an ecosystem that fosters innovation and adaptation.

In conclusion, the relentless march of AI technology in retail operations is rewriting the rules of the game. From supply chain enhancements to dynamic pricing, AI is offering retailers unparalleled opportunities to refine processes, delight customers, and stay ahead of competitors. As retailers harness the power of AI, they'll continue to redefine the operational landscape, pushing the boundaries of efficiency and innovation. The future of retail operations, shaped by AI, promises a horizon of endless possibilities, fostering a new era of retail excellence.

Chapter 2:
Personalized Shopping Experiences

As we delve deeper into the transformative power of AI within retail, personalized shopping experiences emerge as a beacon of innovation, seamlessly intertwining consumer data and cutting-edge technologies. In this ever-evolving landscape, AI crafts unique experiences tailored to individual preferences, reshaping how consumers interact with brands, both online and in physical stores. Imagine walking into a store where your preferences are anticipated, or browsing online with recommendations that feel intuitively aligned with your desires. The magic lies in AI's capacity to analyze and interpret data patterns, creating a nuanced understanding of consumer needs that drives not just engagement but loyalty, paving the way for an era where shopping becomes more than a transaction—it's an experience that feels personally curated for each individual. This shift doesn't merely enhance customer satisfaction but fuels a competitive edge for retailers, urging them to embrace personalization as a core strategy in their quest for relevance and growth in an increasingly demanding market.

Data-Driven Customization

In today's retail landscape, data-driven customization isn't just a buzzword; it's a vital practice reshaping the way businesses understand and cater to their customers. With the advent of AI technology, retailers can now sift through vast oceans of data, honing in on patterns and preferences that were previously impossible to detect. This shift is changing the expectations of consumers, who now desire not just personalization, but a seamless experience that's tailored to their unique tastes and needs.

Consider this: each time someone clicks "add to cart" or even just lingers over a product, a valuable piece of data is created. This data, seemingly insignificant on its own, becomes incredibly powerful as it accumulates. AI technologies harness these troves of information to craft what I like to think of as a "consumer fingerprint"—a digital reflection of a person's unique shopping habits, preferences, and behaviors. This fingerprint allows retailers to predict what a shopper might want before they even know themselves.

Say you're shopping for a new pair of sneakers. In the past, your choices might have been influenced by an array of factors like magazine ads or recommendations from friends. Nowadays, data-driven AI can analyze your previous purchases, the style of sneakers you've browsed, even the time of year, to suggest the perfect pair. It feels as if the retailer knows you as well as a close friend would, offering selections that resonate on a personal level. This isn't just technologically impressive; it's transformative.

One of the most striking benefits of data-driven customization is its ability to deliver relevancy at scale. Retail environments that once struggled to cater to individual preferences can now offer personalized experiences to every single customer—whether in a small boutique or a sprawling digital marketplace. In doing so, they not only enhance the consumer experience but also build brand loyalty and increase conversion rates.

Furthermore, the insights gleaned from data allow businesses to refine their inventory and marketing strategies. By understanding purchasing habits, AI can predict trends and adjust stock accordingly, preventing the dreaded problem of overstocking or stockouts.

Similarly, marketing campaigns become more efficient as retailers target audiences more precisely, enhancing ROI and minimizing waste.

Yet, the journey towards effective data-driven customization isn't without its hurdles. Data privacy concerns loom large, with consumers increasingly anxious about how their data is used. This apprehension necessitates a balance between personalization and privacy, requiring retailers to foster trust by ensuring data is both used ethically and securely.

Moreover, the implementation of this technology can be daunting. Retailers must invest in robust AI platforms capable of processing and learning from massive datasets. It's an investment not just in technology, but in redefining business models to prioritize customer-centric strategies. For many, it requires a cultural shift within organizations, emphasizing data literacy and a willingness to adapt.

Despite these challenges, the potential of data-driven customization to revolutionize the retail experience is undeniable. As AI technologies continue to evolve, so too will the sophistication of personalized shopping experiences. It's not hard to imagine a future where AI anticipates not just our immediate needs but our latent desires, crafting an immersive shopping journey that's both intuitive and inspiring.

Ultimately, data-driven customization marks a pivotal step in the evolution of retail. It represents the remarkable ability of AI to bridge the gap between technological potential and human needs. As retailers harness this power, they don't just transform their businesses; they reshape the way the world shops, setting a new standard for excellence in the consumer's journey.

The Role of AI in Customer Engagement

The retail landscape has undergone a seismic shift with the introduction of artificial intelligence (AI), and nowhere is this change more visible than in customer engagement. In an era where consumers crave personalized experiences, AI serves as a powerful ally for retailers aiming to meet these expectations. It's not just about collecting data; it's about using that data to anticipate needs, suggest products, and create a shopping experience that feels intuitive and bespoke—not that we're using that word here.

The essence of customer engagement lies in understanding the consumer journey. AI technologies have revolutionized this process by leveraging machine learning algorithms and data analytics to create dynamic, personalized paths for shoppers. For instance, AI tools analyze browsing behaviors, past purchases, and even social media interactions to craft suggestions that feel both personalized and serendipitous. This kind of tailored experience increases engagement and drives sales, as customers are more likely to respond positively to suggestions that resonate with their individual preferences and needs.

Moreover, AI doesn't just personalize; it also predicts. Predictive analytics have become an invaluable tool for retailers aiming to engage customers more proactively. By analyzing patterns and trends from large datasets, AI systems can forecast customer behaviors, enabling retailers to offer timely promotions or suggestions before consumers even realize they want them. This preemptive approach enhances the customer experience, making it not only more personalized but also more engaging.

Chatbots, an AI technology, deserve a special mention here. Acting as the friendly face of AI in customer service, they offer immediate responses to inquiries, 24/7 availability, and a seamless integration with other digital channels. By taking on the more routine inquiries, these systems free up human employees to handle complex issues, thus improving overall service quality and customer satisfaction. Furthermore, the natural language processing capabilities of AI are continuously evolving, improving the quality and warmth of these automated interactions.

However, the role of AI in customer engagement extends beyond mere personalization and prediction. It's also critical in building customer loyalty. AI-driven loyalty programs analyze customer purchasing habits and preferences to offer rewards and incentives that truly matter to each individual consumer. This increases the likelihood of repeat purchases and brand loyalty, turning casual shoppers into steadfast brand advocates.

AI's ability to integrate seamlessly with all touchpoints of the consumer journey is critical for omni-channel retail strategies. Whether a customer is shopping online, using a mobile app, or in-store, AI systems ensure that data is synchronized in real-time, providing a cohesive experience that doesn't miss a beat. This ensures uniform engagement at every touchpoint, contributing to greater customer satisfaction and loyalty.

Yet, the use of AI in customer engagement is not without challenges. Concerns about data privacy and security are at the forefront. As AI systems become more adept at collecting and analyzing personal data, retailers must navigate the delicate balance between personalization and privacy. Building trust with customers through transparent data practices and robust security measures is essential.

In this rapidly evolving landscape, the potential for AI to transform customer engagement is vast and largely untapped. As technology advances, the sophistication and capabilities of AI in this realm will only grow, providing retailers with more profound insights and more effective tools to connect with their customers. Those who embrace these changes will find themselves at the forefront of a retail revolution, where customer engagement is both a science and an art.

As we look to the future, it's clear that AI will continue to play a pivotal role in shaping personalized shopping experiences. By seamlessly blending technology with human insight, retailers can foster deeper connections with their customers, transforming the shopping experience from a transactional interaction to a meaningful relationship. The true potential of AI in customer engagement is still emerging, promising a new era of shopping that is as engaging as it is efficient.

Chapter 3:
Inventory Management with AI

Inventory management stands at the forefront of the retail revolution, and AI is the engine driving profound change. By transforming how retailers handle stock, AI introduces a paradigm where real-time data is king. Gone are the days of cumbersome manual checks; now, AI systems ensure that stock levels are continuously monitored with unparalleled accuracy. This leads to smarter, faster decision-making and results in an optimized inventory that's always in tune with consumer demand. With precise forecasting, businesses can predict buying patterns with a level of accuracy that minimizes overstocking and stockouts, saving costs and enhancing customer satisfaction. As these tools become more sophisticated, they're not just about keeping shelves stocked— they're about strategically aligning inventory with the ever-evolving needs of a savvy market, paving the way for retailers to thrive in a competitive landscape. The future of inventory management is not just about managing stock; it's about mastering it through the intelligent use of AI.

Real-Time Stock Monitoring

Inventory management in retail isn't just about counting what's in the warehouse or on store shelves; it's about having the right products at the right time to meet customer demand without overstocking or understocking. Real-time stock monitoring with AI is revolutionizing how retailers manage their inventory, providing the agility and precision required in today's fast-paced market. By employing AI technologies, retailers can now track their stock levels instantaneously, across multiple channels and geographies, ensuring they respond to the ebb and flow of consumer demand with unprecedented speed and accuracy.

The primary advantage of real-time stock monitoring is its ability to provide merchants with up-to-the-minute data on inventory levels. This is achieved through the integration of IoT devices, sensors, and advanced software systems that perpetually track stock movement. AI algorithms then process this information to offer insights that would be impossibly complex for humans to discern manually. For instance, when an item is scanned at a checkout counter or purchased online, AI systems can immediately adjust inventory counts and flag low-stock items for replenishment.

Furthermore, AI-driven stock monitoring isn't just about keeping tabs on the quantity of goods. It empowers retailers with the ability to recognize patterns and predict stock requirements based on a multitude of factors, from historical sales data to regional weather patterns, social media trends, and even local events. This foresight allows businesses to preemptively adjust their stocks, ensuring they're always equipped to meet the demand peaks without excess waste. Retailers are no longer reacting to low inventories; they're anticipating adjustments before shortages occur.

Moreover, real-time monitoring systems can lead to more efficient operations within the retail supply chain. When inventory data is accurately kept and updated in real time, it simplifies tasks like order fulfillment, warehouse management, and logistics coordination. Stock-outs, which can cause severe disruptions and lead to dissatisfied customers, are minimized. AI can forecast the optimal time to reorder products and even automate the replenishment process, greatly enhancing operational efficiency. This not only reduces labor costs associated with manual stock checks but also lessens the likelihood of human error.

Another critical impact of real-time stock monitoring is enhancing customer satisfaction. In an age where consumers expect seamless and instant service, being able to confirm product availability promptly influences purchasing decisions and fosters brand loyalty. By ensuring stock levels are accurately reflected online, and in store, retailers can manage customer expectations better. This transparency enhances the shopping experience, as customers can trust the information they receive about product availability, whether they're browsing online or visiting a physical store.

The integration of machine learning and AI into inventory systems also aids in the evaluation of product performance. Retailers gain access to detailed analytics that identify which products are flying off the shelves and which are stagnating. These insights can guide promotional strategies and tailor marketing efforts to suit consumer preferences more closely. Advanced analytics also help in identifying inventory turnover rates, thereby enabling smarter merchandising decisions.

Furthermore, real-time stock monitoring supports sustainability efforts by significantly reducing waste. By maintaining optimal inventory levels, retailers can cut down on the stock of perishable goods that might otherwise go unsold and ultimately wasted. AI can predict seasonal demand fluctuations, helping retailers align production schedules to market needs. This alignment ensures a more sustainable and environmentally friendly approach to stock management.

However, adopting AI for real-time stock monitoring does come with potential challenges. Integrating AI systems with existing infrastructure can be a complex task requiring significant investment. Retailers need to carefully select technology partners and solutions that align with their specific needs. Moreover, ensuring data security in a system that continuously processes sensitive information is paramount to maintaining consumer trust and compliance with legal standards.

Despite these challenges, the potential rewards of real-time stock monitoring far outweigh the initial hurdles. Businesses willing to invest in this transformative technology will find themselves at a competitive advantage, thanks to heightened efficiency, improved customer satisfaction, and a proactive approach to inventory management. As the technology continues to mature, it is expected to provide even more sophisticated tools and methods for retailers to manage their stocks, shaping the future of commerce in a data-driven world.

In conclusion, real-time stock monitoring is becoming an indispensable component of modern inventory management. Its ability to provide immediate insights into inventory status, coupled with AI's predictive capacities, helps retailers navigate the complexities of today's retail environment. By integrating real-time monitoring, businesses can not only react to current conditions but also anticipate future needs, ultimately delivering a streamlined, efficient, and responsive retail operation. As AI technology progresses, its role in refining retail operations will only grow, paving the way for an era where the right product will always be available at the right time.

Forecasting Demand Accurately

In the whirlwind world of retail, anticipating customer needs is both an art and a science. Achieving an accurate demand forecast is crucial not only for optimizing inventory levels but also for enhancing customer satisfaction. As AI permeates the foundational aspects of retail operations, it brings precision and predictability that were previously unimaginable. Retailers who harness the power of AI-driven demand forecasting can sail smoothly through unpredictable market conditions, ensuring the right products are available at the right time.

Traditionally, demand forecasting involved sifting through past sales data, seasonal trends, and economic indicators. However, these methods often fell short of capturing the nuances of consumer behavior, particularly in a rapidly changing market. Enter AI: with its capability to analyze vast datasets and discern patterns, AI provides a quantum leap in the accuracy of demand forecasts. By integrating machine learning algorithms that learn and adapt over time, retailers are equipped to make better-informed decisions.

Consider this: AI can process and interpret data from myriad sources, including social media trends, economic forecasts, local events, and even weather conditions, to predict demand spikes or dips. This multi-faceted analysis enables retailers to prepare proactive strategies, adjusting inventories before trends peak or recede. The ability to predict demands accurately can mean the difference between profit and loss, especially when critical factors like lead times and inventory storage costs are at play.

Moreover, AI's predictive prowess extends beyond merely stock levels. It can provide insights into pricing strategies, marketing initiatives, and product launches. By aligning inventory with anticipated demand, retailers can reduce overstock or stockouts, minimizing the necessity of markdowns and enhancing gross margins. The real magic, however, lies in AI's ability to learn and improve continuously. As more data flows through the system, its forecasts become increasingly precise, evolving alongside market dynamics.

Human intuition and experience have their limits, especially when analyzing complex datasets. This is where AI shines, integrating intuitive capabilities into algorithms. It's not just about crunching numbers but interpreting human sentiments and behaviors subtly and contextually.

One might wonder, what exactly powers this transformative ability? At the heart of AI-driven demand forecasting are advanced algorithms like neural networks, regression models, and decision trees. These tools facilitate pattern recognition at an unparalleled scale and depth, turning data into actionable predictions. They identify the interdependencies that traditional models often overlook, ensuring a more comprehensive understanding of market behavior.

Let's take the example of neural networks, which mimic the human brain's functioning to identify patterns and correlations amidst seemingly chaotic data. In demand forecasting, they can predict not only how a single product will perform but also how similar products may behave in conjunction. Meanwhile, regression models account for various variables, providing forecasts rooted in statistical significance, while decision trees help visualize possible outcomes based on historical decisions.

Implementation, however, requires careful calibration. Retailers must ensure that the data being fed into AI systems is clean, accurate, and comprehensive. Any anomalies or biases in data can skew forecasts, leading to misguided strategies. Continuous monitoring and updating of data ensure that the AI remains informed and relevant.

The benefits of AI in demand forecasting aren't confined to large retailers with expansive budgets. Even small businesses can leverage AI tools initially designed for larger markets. Today, affordable AI solutions are available that deliver tailored insights to meet the unique challenges faced by smaller retailers, which traditionally might not have had access to such advanced technology.

Despite the automation and tech-savviness of AI, human oversight remains paramount. Knowledge and wisdom derived from years of experience, combined with AI's analytical powers, create a robust forecasting framework. These systems are not perfect and may not account for unforeseen events like global economic shifts or sudden changes in consumer sentiment due to societal factors. Thus, collaboration between AI and human insight ensures a balanced approach to demand forecasting.

We're watching the role of AI in retail usher in a new era, where efficiency and insight become the norm rather than the exception. The competitive edge gained through accurate forecasting translates directly into business resilience and sustainability, particularly in a landscape that's constantly evolving. It's an opportunity to align closer with customer expectations, spawning innovation in not just retail operations but also in customer relations and product offerings.

The progress in AI-driven demand forecasting also heralds deeper implications for retailers' operational workflows. Forecasting accuracy impacts supply chain logistics, influencing timing and delivery routes, and directly ties into how organizations allocate resources. Optimal forecasting ensures not just financial savings but also a reduction in carbon footprints, contributing to sustainability efforts that are increasingly important in modern business practice.

As the narrative of commerce continues to unfold, AI will remain a vital protagonist in navigating the intricacies of demand forecasting. Embracing these tools is not merely a trend but a necessity, a catalyst for change that holds the potential to harmonize supply and demand with unprecedented accuracy.

In sum, forecasting demand accurately with AI is the confluence of technology, data, and human creativity. It's an ongoing journey where the destination is an adaptable, customer-centered retail ecosystem. As we continue exploring AI's growing influence in retail, we uncover novel ways to convert challenges into opportunities, paving pathways to future success and innovation.

Chapter 4:
AI in Supply Chain Optimization

In the bustling world of retail, supply chain optimization emerges as a linchpin to achieving seamless operations, and artificial intelligence (AI) plays a transformative role in this domain. By infusing AI technologies into supply chains, companies unlock unprecedented efficiencies, driving both speed and accuracy in logistics operations. Predictive analytics refine logistical predictions, offering firms a foresight that anticipates disruptions and realigns resources preemptively. This agile adaptability not only curtails costs but also anchors a business's competitive edge in a volatile market landscape. As forward-thinking professionals carve paths through this digital transformation, AI stands as an invaluable partner, transforming supply chains from static, reactive entities into dynamic, proactive networks tailored for future challenges. The result is an ecosystem where data-driven decision-making flourishes, empowering retailers to meet consumer demands promptly and sustainably.

Enhancing Supply Chain Efficiency

In the dynamic world of retail, optimizing supply chains has emerged as a critical focus, driven largely by the capabilities of Artificial Intelligence (AI). The modern supply chain is a complex, multifaceted operation requiring a multitude of decisions each day. At the heart of this transformation is AI's ability to process vast amounts of data and provide actionable insights that were previously unimaginable.

AI technologies have transformed traditional supply chain models into agile, responsive ecosystems. By harnessing machine learning algorithms, companies can now predict potential disruptions before they occur, ensuring greater resilience and adaptability. This proactive stance minimizes downtime and maximizes productivity, allowing retail businesses to maintain continuity in increasingly competitive markets.

Consider the role of AI in automating supply chain processes. Automation, powered by AI, streamlines operations by reducing the need for manual intervention. For example, tasks such as order processing, inventory updates, and shipment tracking are efficiently handled by intelligent systems. This shift not only reduces the margin for error but also allows human workers to shift focus toward more strategic, value-adding activities.

One of the standout features of AI in supply chain efficiency is predictive analytics. By analyzing historical data alongside real-time inputs, AI can forecast demand with remarkable accuracy. This insight is invaluable for inventory management - helping businesses maintain optimal stock levels to meet consumer demand without overstocking, which reduces waste and costs.

Moreover, smart logistics is a game-changer. AI-powered tools optimize shipping routes, ensuring that products are delivered timely and cost-effectively. Advanced algorithms assess multiple variables such as traffic patterns, weather conditions, and delivery timelines to select the most efficient pathways. The outcome? Minimized fuel consumption and reduced carbon footprints, contributing to more sustainable business practices.

Collaboration across various stakeholders in the supply chain is another area where AI shines. Enhanced connectivity and data sharing between suppliers, manufacturers, and retailers lead to improved transparency and collaboration. AI platforms allow these stakeholders to access shared information seamlessly, promoting coordinated decision-making that optimizes the overall supply chain performance.

Consider too, the potential of AI in quality control. Machine learning algorithms can detect patterns and anomalies in production data, signaling potential defects early in the manufacturing process. This capability ensures higher product quality and consistency, reducing returns and enhancing customer satisfaction. Additionally, AI-powered visual inspection systems surpass human capability in precision and speed, further embedding efficiency into the supply chain.

AI's integration into supply chain management systems also fosters a data-driven culture. With comprehensive analytics and insights at their fingertips, decision-makers can identify trends, spot inefficiencies, and launch targeted improvements. This level of insight is instrumental for companies endeavoring to achieve lean operations without compromising service delivery standards.

Supply chain optimization isn't just about technology—it's about a mindset change. Embracing AI requires organizations to foster an innovative culture that encourages persistent learning and adaptation. By doing so, businesses become agile entities capable of evolving alongside technological advancements.

Importantly, AI supports enhanced customer experiences by ensuring that products are available when and where they're needed. The seamless operation of the supply chain directly correlates with customer satisfaction, fostering loyalty and repeat business. Through predictive insights and efficient logistics, businesses are poised to serve their customers more effectively, potentially translating into increased market share and profitability.

Nevertheless, integrating AI into supply chains requires thoughtful implementation. Businesses must navigate challenges such as data quality, legacy system integration, and workforce alignment. Training programs and change management initiatives are crucial for successful adoption, ensuring that employees possess the necessary skills and embrace the technological shift.

In conclusion, enhancing supply chain efficiency through AI is not just about implementing new technologies; it's about reimagining the entire supply chain framework. Retailers prepared to leverage AI strategically and thoughtfully will not only streamline their operations but also gain a competitive edge in a rapidly evolving market. As AI continues to mature, the supply chain of the future is poised to become even more intelligent, responsive, and efficient.

Predictive Analytics for Logistics

In the intricate web of retail supply chains, logistics is the backbone that ensures products flow seamlessly from manufacturers to consumers. But the journey is fraught with uncertainties—demand fluctuations, transportation delays, and inventory management issues are constants in the logistics equation. This is where predictive analytics, powered by artificial intelligence, steps in as a game-changer. By leveraging data insights, AI not only anticipates potential disruptions but also provides strategic recommendations to optimize the entire logistics process.

The essence of predictive analytics lies in its ability to analyze vast amounts of historical data to forecast future outcomes. For logistics, this means predicting delivery times, optimizing shipment routes, and even foreseeing maintenance needs for transportation fleets. By using machine learning algorithms and data mining techniques, predictive analytics transforms data into actionable insights. It's not just about predicting what will happen but understanding why it might happen and how to prevent potential issues.

One of the most significant benefits of predictive analytics in logistics is enhancing the accuracy of demand forecasts. Accurate demand predictions allow retailers to maintain optimal stock levels, reducing both overstock and stockouts. These forecasts are more dynamic and precise, taking into account various factors such as seasonality, market trends, and even social media sentiment. As a result, supply chains become more responsive and resilient, capable of adjusting to real-time changes in demand, thus avoiding costly inefficiencies.

Logistics operations are often stalled by unforeseen hurdles like extreme weather events, strikes, or geopolitical tensions. Predictive analytics provides a foresight into these potential disruptions, offering companies the chance to devise contingency plans before issues arise. This proactive approach reduces downtime and keeps the supply chain moving smoothly, preserving both time and resources. By simulating numerous scenarios, logistics managers can evaluate different strategies and choose the most efficient course of action.

Beyond forecasting and problem-solving, predictive analytics can play a crucial role in cost reduction. Reducing transportation costs remains a priority for many retailers, considering that transportation can account for a significant portion of logistics expenses. Predictive models optimize routes based on real-time traffic data, fuel prices, and vehicle condition, ensuring that deliveries are not only timely but also cost-effective. These optimizations lead to a leaner, more efficient supply chain that operates with minimal waste.

Furthermore, predictive analytics enhances customer satisfaction by ensuring reliable product delivery. In an age where consumers expect speedy and accurate delivery, any delays can lead to discontent and potential loss of business. By predicting delivery times with greater accuracy and transparency, companies can communicate proactively with customers, setting realistic expectations and enhancing brand trust.

The adoption of predictive analytics in logistics also facilitates better collaboration among supply chain stakeholders. By sharing predictive insights across the network, manufacturers, suppliers, logistics providers, and retailers can synchronize operations more effectively. This integrated approach leads to improved coordination and alignment of goals across the supply chain, ultimately resulting in a more cohesive and efficient operational framework.

Incorporating predictive analytics into the logistics sector does pose challenges, primarily around data quality and integration. Ensuring that data across the supply chain is accurate, complete, and accessible is vital for the success of predictive models. Inconsistencies in data can lead to misinformed predictions, so retailers must invest in robust data management practices. Equally important is fostering a culture of data-driven decision-making within organizations to fully leverage the potential of predictive analytics.

As AI continues to evolve, the capabilities of predictive analytics within logistics are also expected to grow. Future innovations could include advanced AI models capable of learning from real-time changes and automatically updating predictions as new data becomes available. The integration of Internet of Things (IoT) devices could further enhance data collection and analysis, providing even richer datasets for predictions.

By embracing predictive analytics, retailers can navigate the complexities of modern logistics with increased agility and confidence. It's not just about keeping the supply chain moving but transforming it into a strategic asset that drives competitive advantage. As retail continues to evolve amidst technological advancements, the retailers who harness the power of predictive analytics will be better positioned to anticipate needs, respond to changes, and deliver superior value to their customers.

Ultimately, predictive analytics in logistics isn't just a tool for efficiency; it's a catalyst for reinvention. As AI reshapes the landscape, it empowers retailers to reimagine their logistics strategies, prioritize sustainability, and meet the ever-increasing demands of the global market with precision and foresight. The future of logistics isn't just predictive; it's transformative.

Chapter 5:
Automating Customer Service

In the ever-evolving retail landscape, automating customer service stands as a beacon of transformation, ushering in a new era of efficiency and personalization. By integrating AI-powered chatbots, retailers can now offer instant and tailored responses to customer inquiries, freeing human agents to handle more complex issues and enabling a seamless customer journey. This automation doesn't just enhance interactions; it creates a robust platform for gathering insights into customer preferences and behaviors. Such data becomes invaluable as it feeds into a continuous loop of improvement in service delivery. The amalgamation of AI in customer service is not merely a forward-thinking trend; it's a testament to the relentless pursuit of excellence, where businesses balance the delicate art of human touch with the efficiency of technology. As these intelligent systems become more proficient and human-like, the distinction between automated and human interaction begins to blur, fundamentally reshaping how retailers engage with their customers and setting a new standard for customer experience in the digital age.

AI-Powered Chatbots

In the ever-evolving retail landscape, AI-powered chatbots have emerged as one of the most transformative tools for automating customer service. These virtual assistants, driven by sophisticated algorithms and natural language processing, are reshaping how businesses interact with their customers. Not only do they promise enhanced efficiency and availability, but they also offer a level of personalized interaction that was previously difficult to achieve at scale.

Chatbots stand out due to their ability to handle a multitude of customer inquiries simultaneously, providing immediate responses around the clock. This always-on availability not only meets the growing consumer expectation for instant gratification but also helps retailers manage customer service more effectively. There's no waiting in line, no need for customers to repeat information, and no limitation on time zones. This results in a seamless experience that aligns with today's fast-paced lifestyle.

Moreover, AI chatbots are skilled in understanding and emulating human interaction. They use machine learning to continuously improve their interactions and better understand the nuances of human language. This capability allows them to handle everything from simple questions about store hours to more complex issues like processing returns or troubleshooting order problems. The more interactions they handle, the more adept they become at mirroring the conversational style customers expect from live agents.

One of the greatest advantages of AI-powered chatbots is their ability to scale personalization. By analyzing customer data, these chatbots can offer recommendations, provide personalized assistance, and even anticipate customer needs. They create a more engaging shopping experience by remembering past interactions and preferences, thus fostering a sense of connection and loyalty that encourages repeat business.

Implementing AI chatbots goes beyond mere technical integration; it represents a strategic shift in how retailers view customer service. They are not just tools but partners in customer engagement strategies. In retail, where competition is fierce and differentiation is key, chatbots can offer that essential edge. By providing consistent and personalized service, they help retailers not only to retain customers but also to elevate their brand image.

However, the deployment of AI chatbots is not without its challenges. Retailers must manage customer expectations and ensure that interactions remain human-like to prevent alienating users. It's crucial to design chatbots that are not only functional but also possess empathy and a conversational tone. Fine-tuning these aspects requires rigorous testing and constant updating to adapt to the changing dynamics of consumer interactions.

Beyond customer service, AI chatbots hold potential for other retail functions like marketing and sales. For instance, they can send out personalized promotions, push notifications about new products, or gather customer feedback. By analyzing user data, they help retailers understand market trends and consumer preferences, thereby informing better business decisions.

The technology behind AI chatbots is continually advancing. Developments in machine learning, AI, and natural language processing promise even more capabilities in the future. As these technologies progress, chatbots will become even more adept at handling complex interactions and executing seamless transactions. The rising popularity of voice-activated shopping assistants also hints at future integrations.

Moreover, the future of chatbots in retail could see them evolve into comprehensive virtual shopping assistants. Imagine a virtual guide that not only helps in making purchases but also in styling outfits, offering care tips for products purchased, or even integrating with smart home devices to suggest restocking items. The endless possibilities suggest a future where chatbots are integral to both the front-end customer experience and back-end efficiency.

In an increasingly digital world, AI-powered chatbots symbolize the intersection of technology and customer experience. For retailers looking to streamline operations without sacrificing customer satisfaction, chatbots offer an immediate and impactful solution. As these systems become more advanced, their role within retail will undoubtedly expand, leading to innovations in how we perceive customer service and shopping as a whole.

Ultimately, the success of AI-powered chatbots rests on their capacity to blend intelligence with intuition. A well-designed chatbot should learn from data while also anticipating human emotions and preferences. By doing so, it creates a retail environment that's not only smarter but also more attuned to the needs of diverse customer bases, thus paving the way for a more connected and personalized future in the commerce industry.

Enhancing Customer Interactions

Automating customer service in retail isn't just about efficiency; it's about enhancing the quality of interactions between companies and their customers. In an era where consumers expect instant gratification and seamless experiences across all touchpoints, leveraging AI to improve customer interactions has become a priority for forward-thinking retailers. By offering more personalized and real-time responses, AI is transforming the way we engage with customers, creating an environment where their needs are anticipated and met with minimal friction.

One of the most significant advantages of using AI in customer service is the ability to provide round-the-clock support. Unlike human agents, AI systems are tireless. This means customers can access information and support at any time, day or night. Such availability enhances customer satisfaction by ensuring that help is always available, even during off-hours, thereby elevating the consumer's overall retail experience.

AI-powered chatbots are at the forefront of this transformation. They don't merely respond to queries but engage in meaningful dialogues. By analyzing past interactions and leveraging natural language processing (NLP), chatbots can understand context and intent, providing more relevant and accurate responses. This capability not only increases efficiency but also creates a more human-like interaction, making consumers feel heard and valued.

Moreover, AI can track and analyze customer interactions in real-time, offering retailers invaluable insights into consumer behavior. By understanding patterns and preferences, companies can fine-tune their approaches, ensuring that each interaction is aligned with customer expectations. This continuous feedback loop allows businesses to improve their service quality constantly and offers a unique competitive advantage in the crowded retail space.

In addition to efficiency and availability, AI enhances personalization, a critical component of modern customer service. AI systems can analyze a vast amount of data points—from previous purchases to browsing history—to tailor interactions and offerings to individual preferences. This level of personalization was once the domain of luxury brands but is now accessible to all, thanks to AI technology.

Imagine a virtual shopping assistant that remembers your size, favorite brands, and color preferences. It can recommend products you might like, remind you of items left in your cart, or alert you to sales on items similar to those you've purchased in the past. This proactive approach to customer service makes shoppers feel understood and appreciated, rather than just another number in the system.

Seamless integration of AI tools with existing customer relationship management (CRM) systems also means that every touchpoint with the customer can be meticulously coordinated. The ability to access centralized data allows AI-driven platforms to offer consistent and cohesive support across different channels—be it social media, email, or in-store kiosks. This omnichannel competence ensures that no matter where a customer interaction takes place, the experience feels unified and personalized.

However, enhancing customer interactions with AI isn't without its challenges. The key lies in maintaining the delicate balance between automation and human touch. While AI excels in handling routine inquiries, complex issues often require empathy and nuanced understanding—a domain where human agents shine. The future of customer service likely involves AI and humans working hand-in-hand, with AI handling the routine, allowing human agents to focus on more complex or sensitive interactions.

Furthermore, AI must continuously learn and adapt to the ever-evolving landscape of customer expectations. This involves constant updates and training of AI models, ensuring they remain relevant and effective. Retailers must invest in the ongoing development of their AI systems to prevent them from becoming obsolete as consumer preferences shift over time.

There are ethical considerations as well. Ensuring data privacy and securing personal information are paramount as AI systems gain access to more intimate details of customer profiles. Transparency in how data is collected and used can help build trust and mitigate concerns over privacy, which is crucial for the continued success of AI initiatives in retail.

Retailers who can navigate these challenges stand to benefit immensely from the capabilities of AI. A carefully orchestrated AI strategy not only enhances customer interactions but also leads to increased customer loyalty, as customers are likely to return to brands that not only meet but anticipate their needs. It fosters a cycle of continuous improvement, as each interaction provides insights that can be used to refine and enhance future experiences.

In conclusion, enhancing customer interactions through AI represents a monumental shift in how businesses engage with their clientele. It's not just about automating processes but elevating the customer experience to new heights. By blending the efficiency and analytical prowess of AI with a commitment to personalization and empathy, the retail industry is poised to redefine customer service for the modern age.

Chapter 6:
The Future of Payments

The evolution of payment systems is racing towards an AI-driven horizon, fundamentally altering the landscape of retail transactions. With AI's capability to process vast amounts of data in mere seconds, payment solutions are becoming faster, smarter, and more secure. As intelligent systems learn consumer habits, they streamline payment processes, predicting preferred methods and even pre-approving purchases for a seamless checkout experience. Stores are now exploring biometric authentication and voice-activated payments, reducing reliance on physical cards or cash, and prioritizing convenience and safety. AI also plays a crucial role in enhancing security measures by detecting fraudulent activities with near-precision, thereby fostering trust in digital transactions. The integration of these advanced systems is not merely a technological upgrade but a necessary step toward reshaping commerce for today's dynamic market participants. The continual evolution of AI in payments promises to not only enhance efficiency but also redefine consumer expectations and business models. The future of payments is here, and it's reshaping the very foundation of how we trade, one algorithm at a time.

AI-Driven Payment Solutions

In today's rapidly evolving retail landscape, artificial intelligence is steadily transforming the way we manage transactions. As consumers increasingly expect seamless and efficient buying experiences, businesses are turning to AI-driven payment solutions to meet these needs. This pivot not only answers the demand for faster, more secure transactions but also sets the stage for an era where personalization and convenience are paramount. AI isn't just a tool; it's becoming a silent partner in shaping the commerce of tomorrow.

One of the most notable contributions of AI to payments is the enhancement of transaction speed and efficiency. Traditional payment systems often require several seconds, if not minutes, to process, leading to bottlenecks and consumer frustration, especially during peak shopping times. AI optimizes this process by utilizing advanced algorithms to manage and process transactions in real-time, significantly reducing the latency associated with traditional payment methods. This immediacy not only enhances the consumer experience but also boosts the retailer's ability to handle higher transaction volumes with ease.

Beyond speed, AI is revolutionizing personalization within payment systems. By leveraging machine learning and big data analytics, AI can analyze consumer behavior and purchasing patterns to recommend optimized payment plans or methods. This means that the system could suggest a preferred payment method based on past behavior, offering tailored user experiences that resonate with individual preferences. In a world where customization is key, this level of personalization can significantly elevate the consumer journey.

Then there's the element of security—a critical concern as digital transactions proliferate. AI-driven payment solutions are raising the bar for fraud prevention and security by implementing intelligent detection systems. These systems utilize deep learning techniques to continuously monitor transactions for irregularities, flagging suspicious activity in real-time and thus preventing fraudulent activities before they can proceed. The application of AI in this context not only decreases the risk of fraud but also reinforces consumer trust in digital payment systems, which is crucial for their widespread adoption.

AI also plays a pivotal role in developing innovative payment methods, like biometric payments and voice-activated transactions. By harnessing AI's ability to process and analyze biometric data, retailers are now beginning to offer payment options that rely on fingerprints, facial recognition, and even voice commands. These innovations don't just suggest a future where plastic cards might become obsolete; they also hint at a world where the entire transaction can be finalized with a mere glance or gesture—ushering in a level of convenience and security that was previously unimaginable.

This shift toward AI-driven payment solutions also supports the growing trend of invisible payments, where the consumer's purchase journey becomes so seamless and integrated that they are barely aware of the transaction occurring. Think of platform environments like Amazon Go, where customers simply pick up items and leave the store, with payments processed automatically via sophisticated AI systems. Such experiences, enabled by AI, transform shopping from a series of conscious decisions into an intuitive and naturally flowing activity.

In another vein, AI is helping retailers optimize their payment ecosystems by analyzing vast amounts of transactional data to arrive at better insights. These insights can guide strategic decisions such as adjusting payment methods accepted or streamlining transaction processes to lower costs. By following such data-informed strategies, businesses are equipped to predict and respond swiftly to changing consumer payment preferences and market trends.

Upgrading to AI-driven payment systems also aligns with cost-efficiency targets for many retailers. Traditional infrastructure often incurs high operational costs due to maintenance and the need for manual oversight. In contrast, AI systems can automate a substantial portion of these tasks, allowing businesses to allocate resources more effectively and reduce overhead costs. Moreover, as AI technologies continue to advance, the cost of implementation is expected to decrease, making it an even more attractive option for retailers of all sizes.

Finally, the integration of AI into payment solutions facilitates better access to global markets by accommodating diverse payment methods and currencies seamlessly. AI can intelligently manage multi-currency transactions, localizing them for different regions and ensuring compliance with varied financial regulations. This capability doesn't just enhance the retailer's global reach but also fortifies the payment system's adaptability to diverse consumer needs across different geographic regions.

In summary, AI-driven payment solutions represent a powerful innovation within the retail sector, offering speed, security, personalization, and global reach in ways that traditional systems cannot. As AI technologies continue to mature and integrate into our daily lifestyles, we'll likely see these systems become even more intuitive and indispensable. For forward-thinking professionals and entrepreneurs, embracing AI in payment solutions isn't just an option; it's becoming an imperative strategy to stay relevant and competitive in the future of commerce. The promise of AI lies not just in what it can do today, but in the boundless possibilities it holds for tomorrow's payments landscape.

Security and Fraud Prevention

In the rapidly evolving landscape of retail payments, securing transactions and preventing fraud have become cornerstones of future-facing strategies. As AI technologies drive innovative payment solutions, the stakes for ensuring data protection and trust have never been higher. It's no longer enough to rely on traditional methods of security; the sophistication of today's threats requires a dynamic and adaptive approach. Businesses must now invest in AI-powered tools that not only detect but predict and prevent fraudulent activities.

AI at the Forefront of Security AI brings a transformative edge to payment security, primarily by enabling real-time threat detection through machine learning algorithms. These algorithms can analyze transactions in milliseconds, identifying unusual patterns that may suggest fraudulent behavior. Unlike human analysts, AI can process vast datasets without fatigue, uncovering insider threats or external breaches before they can materialize into tangible losses. It's a proactive, rather than reactive, strategy that's shifting the dynamics of security in retail.

Moreover, AI systems continuously learn and adapt from each transaction, constantly improving their accuracy and effectiveness. This not only reduces false positives but also enhances customer experience by minimizing unnecessary transaction declines. Through sophisticated behavioral analytics, businesses can offer seamless yet secure shopping experiences, balancing convenience with vigilance: a crucial component in today's consumer-centric market.

Biometrics: A New Layer of Security Biometric authentication, powered by AI, is becoming an integral component of payment systems. Facial recognition, fingerprint scanning, and voice recognition are not just sci-fi visions anymore; they're practical solutions employed by leading retailers to combat fraud. These biometric systems offer an additional layer of security that is exceedingly difficult to replicate, thus serving as a formidable barrier against fraudulent access attempts.

Add to this the element of convenience: customers appreciate the ability to authenticate transactions with a fingerprint or facial scan, simplifying checkout processes without compromising protection.

The convergence of AI and biometrics is setting new standards in the industry, making payments more secure yet remarkably simple.

Fraud Prevention Through Predictive Analytics

Predictive analytics, driven by AI, is another game-changer in the realm of fraud prevention. By analyzing historical data and transaction patterns, predictive models can ascertain the likelihood of fraudulent activities even before they occur. It's akin to having a crystal ball for payments, where businesses can foresee risks and take necessary precautions proactively.

One of the pivotal benefits of this approach is the ability to customize fraud prevention strategies according to individual consumer profiles. The power of AI enables retailers to distinguish between an irregular transaction that's likely fraudulent and a legitimate one, thereby preventing revenue losses while maintaining customer satisfaction. This fine-tuning is essential in an era where personalization is key, but security cannot be compromised.

User Education and Trust Building Technological advancements are only as effective as their implementation and acceptance by the end-users. Therefore, educating consumers about the security measures in place and how they function becomes crucial. Confidence in AI-driven systems is built on transparency—explaining the algorithms' methods and benefits fosters trust and encourages wider adoption.

Engaging informational campaigns and user-friendly interfaces that guide customers through secure transaction processes can alleviate concerns over privacy and fraud, reinforcing brand loyalty in the process. Retailers who excel at blending cutting-edge technology with clear communication are poised to lead in the payments space.

Collaboration: The Backbone of Global Security Combatting fraud is not an endeavor that can be approached in isolation. A collaborative ecosystem, where information is shared between businesses, financial institutions, and even governments, is paramount. AI facilitates this through the exchange of intelligence, making security measures both comprehensive and cohesive across different sectors. It ensures that fraudulent patterns spotted by one entity can be flagged and countered by others, drastically reducing the global footprint of cyber threats.

Additionally, regulatory bodies are beginning to embrace AI as an ally rather than a complication. Regulations and compliance frameworks are evolving with technological advancements, providing room for AI-driven security implementations while ensuring consumer rights are upheld.

The Future of Secure Payments As we envision the future of payments, a secure ecosystem fortified by AI capabilities emerges. The integration of AI in payment systems redefines the battleground against fraud, making transactions safer and reinforcing the trust placed by consumers in digital payment solutions. These advancements not only hold the promise of improved security and privacy but also galvanize innovation, paving the way for novel payment methods that align with futuristic consumer needs.

Ultimately, addressing security and fraud prevention in the context of modern payments is about balancing cutting-edge technology with a human-centric approach. The interplay between AI-driven systems and human oversight ensures that as threats evolve, our defenses do too, creating a future where the integrity of retail transactions is safeguarded. This balance will not only underpin the success of AI-powered retail innovations but also secure their place in the next chapter of commerce.

Chapter 7:
Visual Search and Recognition

In the rapidly transforming retail landscape, visual search and recognition have emerged as powerful tools that tap into the most intuitive of human senses: sight. Utilizing sophisticated AI algorithms, retailers are bridging the gap between seeing and buying, providing customers with an enriched, interactive shopping experience. Gone are the days of tedious keyword searches; now, consumers can simply point their device cameras at objects they desire, triggering immediate product recognition and discovery. This technological advancement not only streamlines the journey from inspiration to purchase but also enhances product recommendations, tailoring them to individual preferences. By analyzing visual data, AI fuels a deeper understanding of consumer behavior and trends, setting the foundation for highly personalized shopping experiences. As we delve into this pivotal transformation, it's clear that visual search and recognition are not just enhancing convenience; they are redefining the very nature of product discovery in the retail realm.

AI for Product Discovery

As we delve into the realm of "Visual Search and Recognition", it's crucial to highlight how AI for product discovery is shaping the future of retail. Imagine walking into a store or browsing online, and not being able to describe precisely what you're looking for. AI-powered visual search comes to the rescue, transforming the way consumers find products and the way retailers understand consumer needs.

With the exponential growth of online retail, consumers are often overwhelmed by the sheer volume of products available. Traditional search methods fall short when shoppers can't articulate their desires through text-based queries. Enter AI's visual search—sophisticated algorithms that allow users to find items simply by uploading a photo. This technology deciphers the image to retrieve relevant product information almost instantaneously, creating a more intuitive shopping experience.

Visual search technology, underpinned by machine learning and deep learning, analyzes images for color, shape, size, and pattern recognition to deliver accurate results. It leverages neural networks to understand and interpret visual data much like the human brain. This ability to process vast datasets of images makes AI an invaluable tool in product discovery, offering up suggestions and alternatives that would have otherwise remained hidden in the depths of extensive product catalogs.

Consider an example: a user spots a celebrity wearing a specific outfit on social media and wants to purchase the same look. Text-based search might yield too many or not enough relevant results. With visual search, they can upload the image, and the AI can identify similar products available for purchase, generating a seamless path from desire to product acquisition.

The implications for retail businesses are profound. Leveraging AI for product discovery not only enhances consumer satisfaction but also boosts conversion rates. By providing users with exactly what they are searching for—often faster than they can with manual searches—businesses increase the likelihood of a sale. It optimizes customer journeys, reduces bounce rates, and encourages repeat visits, creating a win-win scenario for both consumers and retailers alike.

Moreover, visual search opens the door to deeper personalization strategies. Every search query and every engagement with product recommendations contribute to a growing dataset, allowing AI to tailor offerings to individual preferences. As AI gathers and learns from this data, it doesn't just react to consumer interactions; it anticipates them. Over time, this evolves into robust predictive models that can suggest products even before the consumer explicitly expresses a need.

This predictive power also supports cross-selling and upselling strategies. For instance, if a customer often searches for images of casual footwear or similar, the AI can instinctively suggest related accessories like socks or care kits, subtly enhancing the shopping basket value without overwhelming the user with irrelevant choices.

Additionally, AI drives efficiency by harmonizing offline and online shopping worlds. Retailers leveraging visual search can maintain synchronized inventories across platforms, enabling true omnichannel experiences. This integration ensures products discovered through visual means online can also be found in physical stores, creating a seamless transition between browsing and buying, and enhancing the overall customer experience.

The challenges, however, lie in effectively teaching and fine-tuning AI systems. The models need continuous training with diverse datasets to improve accuracy and inclusivity. They must adapt to varying styles, seasonality, and regional aesthetic preferences to provide meaningful results globally. Retailers embarking on this AI journey need to invest in the necessary infrastructure and expertise to harness the full potential of visual search technology.

The rise of AI for product discovery is not only reshaping how consumers search and find products but is pushing the boundaries of what reliable, intuitive retail landscapes look like. With each click, each image, and each discovery, AI is paving the path towards a more connected, responsive, and personalized shopping universe that delights consumers and empowers retailers to thrive in an increasingly digital world.

In conclusion, the evolution of AI in visual search and product discovery is just the beginning of a transformative era in retail. It's a compelling step forward, where images speak louder than words. As retailers harness these technologies, they set the stage for an ecosystem where every consumer interaction is an opportunity to understand, engage, and exceed expectations, driving the commerce landscape toward a future where innovation meets personalization at an unprecedented scale.

Improving Product Recommendations

In retail, the quest for personalizing the shopping experience has been greatly enhanced by technologies in visual search and recognition. This is where AI steps in to redefine how product recommendations are crafted to align more closely with consumer preferences. Imagine a scenario where customers no longer need to search for hours or rely on hit-or-miss techniques to find products they desire. Instead, they can be presented with recommendations that seem to intuitively understand their style and needs, thanks to the capabilities brought about by visual recognition systems.

Visual recognition technology can identify and interpret various elements in images, enabling retailers to analyze consumer preferences on a granular level. This ability goes beyond mere identification and classification of objects, into understanding context, color, style, and even nuances of texture. As a consumer interacts with products through images—perhaps through social media, or by uploading their preferences—AI systems can analyze these visual cues to recommend products that fit their unique tastes. It's not just about showing a similar dress or shoe, but about understanding the intricate details that the consumer is drawn to.

The rise of social media has powered a shift in how consumers discover products, with platforms like Instagram and Pinterest driving visual discovery. Retailers who harness AI-driven visual recognition can capitalize on this trend, creating product recommendation systems that feel natural and intuitive. Products are suggested not merely on browsing history or purchase data, but on a deeper understanding of visual patterns and contextual relevance gathered from the images a consumer interacts with.

Moreover, visual search enhances cross-selling opportunities. When a consumer selects a particular item—be it apparel, furniture, or electronics—AI can suggest products that complement or complete a look or setup. This leads to highly effective bundling strategies and enhances the overall shopping experience. Consider a consumer who uploads a photo of a room; AI can recommend furniture, décor, even color palettes that align with the visible style, potentially increasing purchase likelihood and customer satisfaction.

The sophistication of AI in this domain results in higher-quality recommendations, leading to improved conversion rates and increased basket sizes for retailers. It's akin to an expert stylist knowing just what to pick from a wardrobe to match one's style. This accuracy comes from extensive training models that utilize deep learning to refine their recognition abilities over time, learning not just from individual consumer behavior, but from accumulating patterns across a vast dataset.

While deploying these advanced product recommendation systems, one of the key elements that need consideration is maintaining customer privacy. The data leveraged by visual recognition tools must be collected, stored, and analyzed with robust security measures to prevent breaches and misuse. Retailers need to assure consumers that while AI systems are continually learning from their interactions, the users' data remains confidential and secure.

Another aspect to delve into is the role of machine learning in reducing false positives within visual recognition. Accuracy in product recommendation largely depends on the ability of AI systems to discern correct matches without being misled by anomalies or errors in visual data. Fine-tuning algorithms to interpret customer preferences accurately is an ongoing effort, requiring significant computational power and sophisticated models that can adapt to new information swiftly.

In addition, personalization through visual recommendations creates new pathways for retailers to understand emerging trends and shifting consumer demands. Analysis of visual data can reveal preference patterns which might not be initially apparent in textual or numerical data sources. By incorporating visual intelligence, retailers can gain insights into seasonal trends, colors that attract eyeballs, or even unexpected combinations that resonate with their customer base. This ongoing learning process is crucial for maintaining a cutting-edge retail environment where customer satisfaction is continually optimized.

Ultimately, the integration of visual recognition technology in refining product recommendations signifies a profound shift in how retailers interact with their customers. It's not just about optimizing existing systems but reimagining the customer journey from discovery to purchase. Retailers that efficiently employ AI-driven visual search can create tailored experiences that foster loyalty, drive sales, and capture a greater share of the market.

As technology continues to evolve, so too will the methods for improving product recommendations through AI. Emerging capabilities may include real-time 3D visualization, mixed reality experiences, and even more advanced contextual understanding, all aimed at providing a seamless and enjoyable shopping experience. Retailers must stay attuned to these changes, constantly evaluating and updating their systems to harness the full potential of AI in transforming retail into a more intuitive, delightful, and insightful domain.

Chapter 8:
Dynamic Pricing Strategies

In the ever-evolving landscape of retail, dynamic pricing strategies, powered by AI, have become a game-changer, allowing retailers to navigate the complex world of pricing with unparalleled precision. By leveraging sophisticated algorithms and real-time data analytics, businesses can now set prices that reflect current market demand, competitive positioning, and consumer behavior. This approach not only maximizes revenue and profit margins but also enhances the customer's experience by offering optimal prices at the exact moment of interest. Retailers are increasingly reaping the benefits of AI-driven insights, which continuously adapt to changing conditions such as seasonal trends, inventory levels, and competitor pricing. As a result, they can make informed decisions that keep them ahead of the curve. By harnessing the power of AI for dynamic pricing, retail leaders are not simply reacting to market shifts but strategically positioning themselves to seize opportunities and drive future growth.

AI in Competitive Pricing

In the evolving landscape of retail, pricing isn't just about balancing cost and value—it's a dynamic entity, adapting to rapid market changes and consumer expectations. At the heart of this transformation is AI, reshaping competitive pricing strategies and granting a new edge to forward-thinking retailers. Where there once were static price tags, there's now a digital intelligence capable of learning, predicting, and setting prices with a precision that human intuition alone could scarcely achieve.

AI in competitive pricing is not just about automation; it's about leveraging vast amounts of data to glean insights that were previously inaccessible. This approach allows retailers to understand the competitive landscape in real time. By analyzing competitors' pricing, market trends, and consumer behavior, AI can recommend optimal pricing strategies that maximize both revenue and market share.

The core strength of AI in this domain lies in its ability to process enormous datasets rapidly. While traditional pricing strategies might rely on periodic analyses and historical sales data, AI solutions continuously ingest and process information. This real-time analysis enables retailers to react swiftly to competitors' price changes, demand fluctuations, and emerging market trends, ultimately leading to a more agile and responsive pricing strategy.

AI-driven dynamic pricing opens unprecedented opportunities for personalization. It ensures that customers are presented with prices that reflect real-time market conditions and individual buying behaviors. Instead of a one-size-fits-all approach, AI models can tailor prices to different segments or even individual customers. This level of personalization can enhance customer satisfaction and loyalty, as shoppers feel that they receive fair and relevant offers.

Furthermore, incorporating machine learning algorithms into pricing strategies helps forecast potential outcomes of different pricing scenarios. Retailers can simulate price changes and predict their impact on sales, margins, and consumer perception. By aligning pricing strategies with these predictive insights, retailers can achieve a fine balance between competitiveness and profitability.

One of the most compelling benefits of AI in competitive pricing is its ability to blend multiple data points into cohesive strategies. It doesn't just look at current competitor prices, but also considers factors like seasonal trends, macroeconomic variables, and even the weather. This holistic approach ensures a nuanced understanding of what customers are willing to pay at any given time.

AI technologies also address some of the inherent biases in traditional pricing strategies. Historical data used to inform pricing decisions can often carry biases that reflect outdated market conditions or managerial preconceptions. AI-driven systems, by contrast, focus on current and dynamic patterns, offering less biased solutions grounded in real-time data analysis.

Of course, implementing AI in competitive pricing isn't without its challenges. It requires a significant investment in technology and talent, as well as a cultural shift towards data-driven decision-making. Retailers must ensure that their AI systems are trained on rich, accurate data and are continually updated to reflect changes in market conditions. But those willing to embrace these challenges are likely to find that the return on investment far outweighs the initial hurdles, positioning themselves at the forefront of the retail revolution.

Security and ethical considerations play a pivotal role as well. Retailers must ensure that their use of AI in pricing respects customer privacy and complies with regulatory standards. Transparent pricing practices help build consumer trust, and it's imperative that AI-driven strategies maintain integrity in both the data used and the outcomes achieved.

Despite potential obstacles, the promise of AI in competitive pricing is undeniable. As more retailers adopt these technologies, we can expect an evolved retail ecosystem where prices are more reflective of genuine market forces and consumer demand. The capacity for adaptive pricing not only levels the playing field for retailers of all sizes but also enhances the consumer omnichannel experience by providing consistent yet dynamic pricing across platforms.

The era of AI in competitive pricing is setting a new standard for customer engagement and revenue management. In a marketplace that increasingly values personalization, agility, and efficiency, AI enables retailers to meet these demands with unprecedented acuity. As AI continues to evolve, it will only enhance its role in setting competitive pricing strategies that benefit both the retailer and the consumer, paving the way for a more intelligent and responsive retail environment.

Algorithms for Price Optimization

In the ever-evolving landscape of retail, the ability to dynamically adapt pricing strategies is more critical than ever. As technology advances, retail professionals face the daunting task of cutting through vast and complex data to make informed pricing decisions. This is where algorithms for price optimization come into play, a cornerstone of dynamic pricing strategies. The field is driven by the need to balance competitive pricing with maximizing profit margins, a challenge that grows more acute in today's global economy.

Price optimization algorithms are not just about responding to competitors' prices; they're about interpreting a wide range of variables that influence purchasing decisions. These include consumer behavior patterns, demand fluctuations, inventory levels, and even socioeconomic factors. Algorithms leverage data from both internal sources—like historical sales and inventory data—and external sources, such as real-time competitor pricing and economic indicators, to refine their pricing models continuously.

At the heart of price optimization is machine learning. By using a variety of algorithms ranging from linear regression to complex neural networks, retailers can forecast demand and understand elasticity—how sensitive a product's demand is in relation to its price. This leads to dynamic pricing, where prices aren't static but fluctuate based on calculated predictions to maximize revenue or market share.

Take, for instance, a machine learning algorithm used for optimizing prices in the apparel industry. This algorithm can analyze trends and seasonality in the data, providing insights into how certain color palettes might dominate sales during specific periods. By applying regression analysis and clustering algorithms, retailers can effectively categorize products and predict the right price points to boost sales while avoiding surplus inventory.

Moreover, reinforcement learning is paving the way for smarter, more adaptive pricing mechanisms. Unlike supervised learning, which relies heavily on historical data, reinforcement learning models the environment in real-time and makes decisions that adapt to new market conditions on the fly. This means a retailer's algorithm can learn through a series of trials and feedback loops to identify the optimal pricing strategy over time.

While traditional algorithms have relied on static data inputs, the latest advancements integrate real-time data streaming, making the pricing process faster and more responsive to market dynamics. Technologies like cloud computing and big data analytics enhance the ability to process and analyze data at unprecedented speeds, allowing agile responses to fluctuating market conditions.

Connecting data inputs to predictive outputs requires accurate fine-tuning of algorithms. This is where parameter optimization becomes indispensable. It's about balancing the variables that affect pricing strategies to find the sweet spot for any particular set of conditions. Fine-tuning is akin to personalizing pricing models in much the same way AI tools personalize user content. It ensures that models adapt seamlessly with market trends, pushing decision-making capabilities to new levels.

When discussing price optimization, one can't overlook the ethical considerations involved in using AI-driven approaches. Algorithms must be transparent, and decision criteria should be free from bias. This is particularly important to ensure consumer trust and avoid potential backlash over perceived unfair pricing. Developing algorithms that are not only efficient and profitable but also ethical is an evolving field that requires constant vigilance and adaptation.

Another key factor in algorithmic price optimization is ensuring that models are scalable across multiple markets. A strategy that works well in North America might not necessarily translate to success in Europe or Asia. Different regions have varied consumer behaviors, competitive landscapes, and regulatory frameworks. Therefore, algorithms need to be customized and adaptable to reflect these diverse factors.

Forward-thinking companies are incorporating AI-driven price optimization into their foundational strategies to capitalize on new software capabilities. They aren't just reacting to pricing shifts but strategically engineering them, leveraging predictive analytics and machine learning to steer the market in their favor. The transition from traditional pricing strategies to algorithm-based systems marks a significant shift in how businesses approach commerce.

The profound impact of algorithm-driven pricing strategies signifies a new era where technology doesn't just augment decision-making processes; it actively transforms them. In this landscape, retailers who harness the power of AI for price optimization unlock potential competitive advantages, shaping not just their commercial success but also influencing broader market trends.

As we stand on the cusp of technological advancements, it's crucial to continue exploring and enhancing these algorithmic models. They will undoubtedly play a pivotal role in defining the retail industry's trajectory, helping businesses navigate the complexities of a fast-paced, data-dominated marketplace, ultimately elevating the shopping experience on a global scale.

Chapter 9:
AI and Smart Stores

Smart stores, powered by AI, are reshaping the retail landscape by offering an innovative blend of advanced technologies and consumer-centric experiences. In these environments, AI seamlessly integrates with the Internet of Things (IoT), transforming ordinary shopping trips into interactive journeys. Imagine a store where digital mirrors suggest outfits based on your preferences and body type or shelves that monitor inventory and alert staff when stocks run low. This isn't the future—it's happening now, making shopping more efficient and personalized than ever. The technology-enhanced environment not only improves operational efficiency but also amplifies the customer experience, creating an ecosystem where every touchpoint feels intuitive and connected. By harnessing AI, retailers can anticipate customer needs, optimize product placement, and streamline checkout processes, ensuring a frictionless shopping experience. Smart stores are not just about convenience; they represent a paradigm shift in how consumers engage with retail, moving towards a future where technology empowers both shoppers and retailers to create ongoing value.

Technology-Enhanced Shopping Environments

At the heart of the retail transformation is the evolution of shopping environments. Technology is not just supporting; it's redefining how people shop. With AI pushing the boundaries of retail innovation, brick-and-mortar stores are turning into immersive digital ecosystems. These environments are marked by a seamless blend of physical and digital experiences, creating a new dimension of interactivity and personalization. In this rapidly evolving landscape, retailers are using technology to make shopping not only efficient but also engaging and memorable.

Smart stores are increasingly adopting AI tools to gather real-time insights into customer preferences and behaviors. By integrating AI algorithms, stores can analyze huge datasets on customer movements, product interactions, and purchasing patterns. This data helps retailers craft personalized in-store experiences that resonate with individual shoppers. For instance, digital displays update instantly based on who's in the store, showcasing products that align with the shopper's style and history. These dynamic displays aren't just about aesthetics; they're an integral part of a personalized shopping journey.

Imagine walking into a store where the moment you step in, an AI agent recognizes you through facial recognition technology, welcoming you by name. Instantly, your favorite selections are highlighted on digital panels, and personalized discounts are sent to your phone. This is no longer just a vision; it's a reality in many stores today. Retailers leverage these interactions to build stronger customer relationships, offering a new level of service that distinguishes them from traditional shopping experiences.

Technology-enhanced environments aren't limited to customer interaction; they also revolutionize inventory management. AI systems continuously monitor stock levels, predicting demand fluctuations, and automating reordering procedures. This not only ensures that popular items are always available but also helps in optimizing shelf space through smart shelving solutions. When inventory is managed intelligently, the efficiency translates to a more fluid shopping experience for consumers, reducing the frustration of unavailable products.

Furthermore, these smart environments use AI to enhance staffing efficiencies. AI-driven analytics help in determining optimal staffing levels, ensuring that employees are available when and where they're needed most. By analyzing foot traffic and customer interactions, AI systems can predict peak times, allowing retailers to schedule staff more effectively. This focus on efficiency extends beyond employee management to operational sustainability, as resource usage is optimized further.

One of the groundbreaking advancements in smart stores is the application of augmented reality (AR). AR technologies blend digital content with the physical world, allowing customers to visualize how products will look in their homes without leaving the store. Through AR devices or applications, shoppers can engage in 3D visualizations, try virtual clothing, or even see how furniture pieces fit into their living spaces. This brings the online and offline worlds closer, offering customers more informed decision-making capabilities right at their fingertips.

The integration of the Internet of Things (IoT) into retail settings further amplifies the potential of technology-enhanced environments. IoT devices, such as smart shelves and beacons, communicate with customers' smartphones to deliver promotions and product information directly. This constellation of connected sensors allows retailers to gather detailed data, track customer preferences, and even monitor environmental conditions inside the store. The result is a hyper-connected ecosystem that provides a truly customized shopping experience.

Digital mirrors and smart fitting rooms exemplify the next level of personalization. These tech-savvy solutions allow customers to try on clothes virtually, adjusting sizes and outfits with simple gestures. The smart fitting room suggests accessories and completer looks based on what the shopper tries, leveraging AI to recommend complementary products. This interactive and engaging experience not only delights the customer but also encourages more purchases with confidence.

Sustainability has become a crucial component of modern retail strategies. AI and technological innovations in smart stores contribute significantly to greener practices by analyzing energy consumption patterns and optimizing resource usage. From controlling lighting and temperature to waste management, these advanced systems help reduce a store's environmental footprint. Retailers committed to sustainability see technology's role as essential in driving their environmental initiatives forward.

Beyond enhancing the customer experience, technology-enhanced shopping environments foster innovation. They serve as testbeds for pioneering concepts like robotic assistants and autonomous checkout solutions. Retailers experimenting with robotic technology find it reshapes customer interaction, while autonomous checkout systems drastically reduce queuing times, enhancing convenience for the shopper. These breakthroughs are setting new standards in how transactions occur within retail spaces.

The continuous evolution of these environments underscores the profound effect technological advancements have on consumer expectations. Customers no longer walk into a store merely to browse; they seek interactive experiences that blend seamlessly with their digital lives. For retailers, this means adopting a proactive approach to innovation and staying ahead of tech trends that redefine shopping practices.

In conclusion, technology-enhanced shopping environments signify a paradigm shift in the retail industry. Retailers willing to adapt and invest in cutting-edge solutions are setting themselves apart in a competitive landscape. As AI and associated technologies further permeate retail, their role in redefining how we shop becomes increasingly pivotal. The future is a smart, experiential journey where the lines between physical and digital realms blur, crafting unforgettable shopping experiences for consumers worldwide.

The Role of IoT in Retail

The integration of the Internet of Things (IoT) in retail is like adding another layer of intelligence that embarks on enhancing the traditional retail experience. In essence, IoT connects everyday objects to the internet, providing retailers with unprecedented access to data and insights. This interconnectedness holds the potential to revolutionize various facets of the retail environment by streamlining operations, improving customer experiences, and pioneering new business models.

IoT devices are transforming retail spaces into smart stores by integrating technology seamlessly into consumer touchpoints. For instance, smart shelves, equipped with weight sensors and RFID tags, offer real-time inventory data, enabling retailers to efficiently manage stock levels and reduce shortages or overstock situations. This real-time data not only helps in maintaining inventory but also offers insights into consumer behavior and preferences, allowing retailers to tailor their product offerings effectively.

In parallel, IoT brings a new dimension to personalized shopping experiences. By using sensors and beacons, retailers can now track customer movements within stores, gather data on shopping patterns, and deliver personalized messages or offers directly to consumers' smartphones. This level of personalization enriches the shopping journey, potentially increasing customer satisfaction and loyalty.

Moreover, IoT enhances operational efficiency within the supply chain. Smart tags and GPS devices can monitor products' location and condition throughout the shipping process, ensuring timely deliveries and minimizing losses or damages. These detailed insights make it possible to innovate in logistics, ultimately reducing costs and improving service quality.

Security is another pivotal area where IoT contributes significantly to retail. Smart cameras and sensors can enhance store security by providing advanced surveillance and monitoring capabilities. These devices can detect unusual behavior or security breaches in real-time, allowing for immediate response and prevention of potential thefts or damages.

The evolution of kiosk technologies powered by IoT is another intriguing development. Interactive kiosks equipped with IoT capabilities can serve as informational hubs within stores, offering product details, reviews, and even making it possible to order items not available in-store. This merger of physical and digital realms effectively expands the store's offerings without the need for physical stock, providing a competitive edge.

Beyond physical stores, IoT's role in enhancing the omnichannel experience is substantial. By providing seamless integration across various platforms, IoT ensures a consistent and integrated customer experience whether shopping online, on mobile, or in-store. This synergy between channels helps retail brands to maintain continuity and engagement with consumers at every touchpoint, fostering a holistic shopping journey.

While the benefits of IoT in retail are profound, there are challenges to navigate. Ensuring data security and consumer privacy is paramount as IoT devices collect and transmit vast amounts of sensitive information. Retailers must invest in robust cybersecurity measures and transparent privacy policies to gain and maintain consumer trust.

Another consideration is the integration of IoT devices into existing systems. Retailers must strategically plan and execute the integration process to avoid disruption in operations. The coordination among IoT solutions, AI technologies, and traditional retail infrastructures can pose technical challenges that require innovative problem-solving approaches.

Despite these challenges, the potential of IoT in reshaping the retail landscape is immense. By leveraging the data and insights provided by IoT, retailers can create more responsive, customer-centric spaces reflecting the dynamic needs of today's consumers. As IoT technology continues to evolve and mature, it promises to offer even greater possibilities for optimizing every aspect of the retail industry, laying the groundwork for a smarter, more connected future.

Chapter 10:
Virtual and Augmented Reality

As we navigate the evolving landscape of retail, virtual and augmented reality (VR and AR) stand out as transformative technologies, reshaping how consumers engage with brands and products. VR immerses shoppers in digitized environments, allowing them to explore stores without leaving their homes, while AR brings products to life in their real-world settings, enhancing both online and in-store experiences. These technologies break down geographical barriers, offering tailored, interactive experiences that were previously unimaginable. Retailers are harnessing VR and AR to craft personalized journeys, captivating customers with virtual try-ons, immersive product demonstrations, and interactive displays that merge the digital and physical realms. In an industry driven by experience and innovation, VR and AR enable brands to connect with their audience on a deeper level, creating memorable interactions that drive engagement and loyalty. As AI continues to refine these technologies, the potential for VR and AR in retail remains boundless, promising a future where shopping becomes not just a necessity but a captivating adventure.

VR and AR in Customer Experiences

Incorporating virtual reality (VR) and augmented reality (AR) into customer experiences is reshaping how we interact with retail environments. These technologies act as powerful bridges between physical and digital realms, offering retailers innovative ways to engage with consumers. The impact is profound, and, in many ways, it signals a transformative shift in how retail will be conducted in the years to come.

VR creates immersive experiences by simulating entire environments for users. Imagine a scenario where customers can explore a luxury boutique from the comfort of their homes, walking through a sprawling showroom, touching products virtually, and even trying them on like they would in a physical store. By leveraging VR, brands offer an engaging and personalized shopping journey that transcends geographical boundaries, rewriting the notion of conventional commerce.

Conversely, AR overlays digital information onto the real world, enhancing the consumer's perception of their environment. Retailers use AR to add layers of information about products, allowing customers to visualize items in their own settings. For instance, furniture retailers enable customers to place life-sized 3D models of sofas or tables in their living rooms using their smartphones, thereby aiding decision-making through highly personalized experiences.

This convergence of technology opens up a plethora of possibilities. For apparel brands, AR lets customers virtually try on clothes. They can see how an outfit looks and fits before making a decision. This possibility not only elevates the shopping experience but also reduces the likelihood of product returns, a common challenge in online retail. It transforms the consumer's journey from a transaction-focused activity into an experience-centric exploration, deepening customer engagement.

Retailers are creatively leveraging VR and AR to offer more than just a glimpse of their products. Take the automotive industry, for example, which uses VR for virtual test drives. Shoppers can experience driving a car on various terrains and conditions without setting foot outside. This use of VR enriches the buying process, making it not just about the product but the lifestyle it promises.

Technology-driven experiences supported by VR and AR are not just limited to try-ons and simulations. These tools also enhance storytelling, allowing brands to weave narratives around their products. In-store experiences with AR offer immersive brand stories that capture the shopper's imagination. These experiences are no longer passive; instead, customers become active participants in the brand narrative, creating emotional connections that transcend traditional marketing methods.

From the retail perspective, integrating these technologies into customer experiences requires a strategic approach. First, it demands an understanding of customer pain points and the identification of moments where VR and AR can add the most value. Whether it's navigating complex product information or reducing friction points in the decision-making process, a thoughtful VR/AR strategy aligns with the customer journey, building loyalty and fostering lifetime value.

Retailers are not alone in this journey. There is a vibrant ecosystem of technology providers who specialize in VR and AR solutions tailored for retail needs. These partnerships allow retailers to access cutting-edge technology without the burden of developing it in-house, making it feasible for businesses of all sizes to experiment with and implement these innovations.

As VR and AR continue to evolve, so does their potential impact on the retail landscape. One of the exciting future directions is their integration with AI to facilitate real-time personalization. Imagine an AI-driven virtual assistant that guides the shopper through a virtual store, offering tailored advice and answering questions in real time based on the customer's preferences and history. This level of personalization is the pinnacle of retail experience, making consumers feel valued and understood.

However, with all these opportunities come challenges. There are concerns regarding data privacy, especially when these technologies are used to gather consumer insights. While the data can refine personalized experiences, it's imperative for retailers to adhere to ethical considerations, ensuring transparent data practices that build and maintain consumer trust.

The implementation of VR and AR also poses logistical challenges. Retailers must invest in the right infrastructure, including high-speed internet and quality hardware, to ensure that these experiences are seamless and effective. As the costs continue to decrease and the technology becomes more accessible, these barriers will likely diminish, paving the way for wider adoption.

Ultimately, the deployment of VR and AR in customer experiences represents a dynamic frontier in retail. These technologies are more than just tools; they're orchestrators of unique and memorable experiences that cater to the desires and expectations of modern consumers. As they continue to blend the imaginary with reality, they hold the potential to redefine not just stores, but the very essence of what it means to shop.

For forward-thinking professionals, entrepreneurs, and tech enthusiasts, understanding and capitalizing on VR and AR could be the key to thriving in the rapidly evolving retail landscape. By embracing these technologies, they're not only revolutionizing how customers shop but also setting new benchmarks for creativity and innovation in the industry.

Enhancing Online Shopping with AR

Augmented Reality (AR) has emerged as a transformative force in online shopping, offering retailers a unique tool to bridge the gap between physical stores and digital experiences. At its core, AR integrates digital information with the user's environment in real time, creating a composite view that enhances consumer engagement and satisfaction. For forward-thinking professionals in the retail industry, understanding the strategic application of AR can unlock new opportunities in customer interaction and sales growth.

One of the most compelling benefits of AR in online retail is its ability to offer a tangible experience, something once thought exclusive to brick-and-mortar stores. Imagine a customer shopping for furniture online; with AR, they can place a digital representation of a sofa in their living room using just their smartphone. This feature not only alleviates the uncertainty of buying without seeing the product in situ, but it also boosts consumer confidence, potentially reducing the rate of returns and exchanges.

Moreover, AR creates a venue for experimentation. Customers often hesitate to purchase items like clothing or accessories online due to sizing and style concerns. AR enables virtual try-ons, allowing shoppers to see how an outfit or a pair of glasses will look before committing to a purchase. This capability caters to the growing consumer desire for interactive and personalized shopping experiences, directly influencing their buying decisions.

Retailers utilizing AR can significantly impact customer retention by fostering a deep emotional connection to their brands. When customers interact with AR applications, they are more likely to remember the experience and the brand providing it. This type of engagement is crucial in a crowded e-commerce landscape where differentiation is key. Consequently, AR can serve as a powerful branding tool, cultivating loyalty through immersive and enjoyable consumer interactions.

Integrating AR into online shopping isn't just about enhancing the customer experience. It's also a valuable means of gathering data on consumer preferences and behaviors. As shoppers interact with AR features, businesses can track their engagement patterns to gain insights into their interests and purchasing habits, empowering retailers to make data-driven decisions. These insights can then inform product development, marketing strategies, and inventory management.

Despite the clear advantages, adopting AR in online shopping comes with its set of challenges. The technology requires significant investment in both hardware and software, as well as skilled professionals to develop and maintain these systems. Retailers must be strategic in choosing AR solutions that offer the most value to their particular market segment, ensuring a return on investment that's justified by enhanced customer satisfaction and increased sales.

For entrepreneurs and tech enthusiasts, the rapid advancements in AR present an exciting opportunity for innovation. As AR technology continues to evolve, its applications in retail will likely expand, encompassing more sophisticated virtual showrooms, interactive tutorials, and even real-time customer service interactions. Visionary businesses will harness these advancements to create seamless, engaging, and rewarding shopping experiences that align with consumers' growing digital expectations.

In light of these possibilities, it's evident that the integration of AR into online retail is more than a trend—it's a long-term enhancement of the shopping experience. As such, retailers must remain adaptable, continuously refining their digital strategies to incorporate new AR features. This agility will not only help them stay relevant but also transform them into leaders in the digital retail space.

The transformative potential of AR in online shopping cannot be overstated. By bridging the sensory gap between physical and online shopping, AR has the capacity to significantly enhance the retail experience. It allows consumers to visualize their purchases more concretely, leading to more informed decision-making and greater satisfaction. For retail businesses, this means not only increased efficiency in converting sales but also building a stronger, more connected customer base. As technology continues to advance, the line between virtual and reality will only continue to blur, creating endless possibilities for those ready to seize them.

Chapter 11:
Managing Consumer Data

As we delve into the complex world of consumer data management, the profound responsibility of harnessing data with care becomes strikingly apparent. In today's data-driven retail landscape, enterprises have a wealth of consumer information at their fingertips, offering unprecedented opportunities to enhance customer experiences. Yet, with great power comes great responsibility; maintaining consumer trust necessitates a rigorous approach to data privacy and protection. Protecting this data is not just a legal obligation but a moral one—redefining the essence of consumer-company interactions. It requires balancing the fine line between personalization and privacy, ensuring that data use is conducted ethically and transparently. By adopting robust AI mechanisms, businesses can both safeguard consumer information and leverage its insights to tailor experiences that respect individual privacy while fostering deeper brand loyalty. Navigating these dual objectives effectively will shape the future trajectory of retail, laying the groundwork for sustainable, trust-based consumer relationships in this era of digital transformation.

Privacy and Data Protection

In the rapidly evolving landscape of AI-driven retail, managing consumer data is both a privilege and a responsibility. As technology continues to enhance the retail experience, privacy and data protection have become essential pillars within this ecosystem. It's no longer a backend concern; it's a core component of establishing and maintaining trust with customers.

As retailers collect a vast amount of consumer data to personalize experiences and streamline operations, the importance of safeguarding this data cannot be overstated. Consumers are increasingly aware of how their information is used, and they're demanding more transparency and control. For retailers, this means implementing robust data protection measures isn't just about compliance; it's a competitive advantage.

At the heart of privacy and data protection in retail is the balance between leveraging data for enhanced consumer experiences and respecting individual privacy rights. Retailers must navigate this complex landscape carefully, understanding that with great power comes great responsibility. Maintaining customer trust hinges on the ability to protect their data while providing value-driven interactions.

Privacy laws such as the General Data Protection Regulation (GDPR) in Europe and the California Consumer Privacy Act (CCPA) in the United States highlight the need for data accountability and transparency. These regulations require retailers to be proactive in their data handling practices, ensuring that consumer data is collected, processed, and stored in a way that respects the user's rights and expectations.

The implementation of these regulations necessitates a multi-faceted approach: from data encryption and secure servers to transparency in data collection and management. Retailers must ensure that their data practices are aligned with both legal requirements and consumer expectations. It's not just about avoiding legal pitfalls; it's about fostering a culture of respect and transparency.

The concept of data minimization is a useful guiding principle for privacy-conscious retailers. By collecting only the data that's truly necessary for a given purpose, retailers can reduce the potential impact of data breaches and misuse. This practice not only aligns with privacy regulations but also builds consumer trust by demonstrating a commitment to protecting their privacy.

Moreover, as AI technologies advance, the challenge is ensuring that these systems are designed with privacy considerations in mind. This involves integrating privacy-by-design principles into AI system development, ensuring that data protection is a core component of AI solutions from the ground up. This proactive approach to privacy can position retailers as leaders in ethical AI deployment.

Yet, privacy and data protection aren't solely about technology and legal frameworks; they're deeply human issues. Retailers need to engage with consumers openly about their data practices. By providing clear and accessible information about how data is used, retailers can empower consumers to make informed choices about their privacy.

In addition to transparency, offering consumers control over their data is a critical aspect of privacy and data protection. This can be achieved through user-friendly interfaces that allow consumers to manage their data preferences easily. Providing options for users to opt-out of data collection or request data deletion is not just a regulatory requirement; it's a way to respect consumer autonomy.

As retail companies harness AI to enhance customer interactions, the risk of potential data breaches increases. Retailers must develop comprehensive cybersecurity strategies that guard against unauthorized data access and ensure the integrity of their systems. Regular audits and updates to security measures are essential in a landscape that's continuously targeted by cyber threats.

Training employees on privacy and data protection is another vital layer of defense for retailers. Educating staff on best practices and making them aware of potential risks can prevent accidental data breaches and ensure that everyone in the organization prioritizes consumer privacy.

The intersection of AI, data privacy, and ethics invites a thoughtful exploration of how algorithms affect consumer data. In the pursuit of personalization, predictive analytics, and automated decision-making, retailers must evaluate how these technologies impact individual privacy. Are biases being introduced into AI systems during data processing? Are there unintended consequences that might affect consumer trust?

Finally, building a culture of privacy and data protection requires continuous dialogue and collaboration among stakeholders across the retail landscape. This includes technologists, legal experts, customer service, and most importantly, consumers. By fostering an environment that prioritizes ethical data practices, retailers can lead by example and encourage industry-wide standards.

In conclusion, the journey of managing consumer data in AI-empowered retail is as much about advancing technology as it is about maintaining the humanity and ethics at its core. By embracing privacy and data protection as foundational elements, retailers can create a future where technology serves not just business goals but also upholds the rights and trust of every consumer.

Ethical Considerations in AI

The integration of artificial intelligence into retail has significantly transformed how consumer data is managed. As AI technologies continue to develop and redefine the retail landscape, ethical considerations around data use become ever more critical.

Understanding these considerations can ensure that AI-driven retail practices benefit businesses and safeguard consumer trust.

The fundamental ethical issue with AI in managing consumer data revolves around privacy. Retailers collect vast amounts of personal data to create personalized shopping experiences, target marketing strategies, and streamline operations. While these efforts enhance customer satisfaction and operational efficiency, they can also lead to potential invasions of privacy if data is not handled responsibly. Retailers must establish strict data governance practices, ensuring that personal information is collected with consent, anonymized where possible, and securely stored to protect against breaches.

Transparency is another cornerstone of ethical AI deployment in retail. Consumers have a right to know how their data is collected, processed, and used. Organizations should adopt transparent practices that enable consumers to understand the scope of data collection and the AI technologies implemented. By being upfront about these practices, retailers can build greater trust with their customers, fostering a relationship based on openness rather than suspicion.

Aside from privacy and transparency, there is the ethical consideration of bias in AI algorithms. AI systems learn from the data they are fed, and if that data is biased, the algorithms can perpetuate or even amplify those biases. In retail, this could translate into unfair treatment of certain consumer groups, affecting pricing, personalized offers, or even customer service interactions. Therefore, it's crucial for retailers to regularly audit their AI systems and data sources to identify and rectify any biases.

Another aspect of ethical AI use is the question of consent. Often, consumers may not fully understand or may inadvertently agree to the terms of data usage when interacting with retail platforms. Retailers must prioritize clear, informative consent processes that genuinely inform consumers about how their data will be used and give them real choices. This involves crafting concise yet comprehensive privacy notices and opt-in mechanisms that don't mislead or confuse the users.

The ethical utilization of AI also demands a balance between innovation and regulation. As AI capabilities advance, regulatory frameworks need to evolve to address new ethical dilemmas that emerge. Retailers must stay informed about both current and upcoming regulations to ensure compliance. Engaging with policymakers and participating in public discourse about AI ethics in retail can help shape fair and effective regulations that protect consumers while allowing for technological progress.

Moreover, the ethical dimension of AI in consumer data management extends to the broader implications of its deployment on society. AI can disrupt job markets, influence consumer choices, and alter market dynamics, raising questions about fairness and equity. Retailers have a responsibility to consider these broader societal impacts when implementing AI technologies. They should strive to ensure that the benefits of AI are distributed fairly across various stakeholders and not concentrated in the hands of a few.

In conclusion, ethical considerations in AI for managing consumer data are multifaceted and demand a proactive approach. Retailers must not only comply with legal requirements but also adopt an ethically sound framework that prioritizes consumer trust, transparency, and fairness. By doing so, they can harness the full potential of AI to create enriched shopping experiences while maintaining the integrity and trust of their customer base.

Chapter 12:
Content Creation and Curation

In the evolving retail landscape, AI is forging a transformative path for content creation and curation, reshaping how businesses connect with their audiences. By harnessing the power of AI, retailers can craft personalized content that resonates deeply with individual consumers, driving engagement and fostering loyalty. This personalized approach not only enhances retail marketing strategies but also allows businesses to deliver messages that are both timely and relevant. AI's ability to analyze vast data sets enables a sophisticated understanding of consumer preferences and behaviors, allowing for the creation of content that's not just engaging but also strategically tailored. As a result, AI empowers retailers to curate experiences that captivate their audience, ensuring that every interaction is meaningful and memorable. The future of retail marketing shines brightly with the promise of AI, offering a dynamic frontier where creativity meets precision in an unprecedented way.

AI for Personalized Content

In the world of retail, the ability to connect with consumers on a deeply personal level has become a game-changer. Personalization, once a mere buzzword, is now a staple strategy, and it's AI that's at the heart of this transformation. It acts like an attentive shopkeeper, who not only knows a customer's name but also understands their preferences, needs, and even their future desires. As the digital age empowers consumers to expect more from their shopping experiences, AI stands as the most versatile tool for retailers to meet those expectations, offering a highly personalized journey for each individual.

AI for personalized content allows retailers to tailor their communications and offerings in real-time, delivering unique shopping experiences across digital and physical platforms. This isn't limited to recommendations in online stores; it extends to email marketing, social media ad targeting, and even the structure of a store's website. AI analyzes consumer data at incredible speeds, sifting through browsing histories, past purchases, and even social media interactions. It builds a sophisticated understanding of each shopper, allowing businesses to create content that resonates on a personal level.

The capability of AI to facilitate personalized content starts with its powerful algorithms. Machine learning models can analyze vast chunks of data to identify patterns in consumer behavior. Imagine a shopper who frequently purchases running gear; an AI system could suggest personalized content like related articles on improving running form or promotions for the latest sneakers. This kind of content isn't just intended to make another sale; it's about creating a connection. By offering relevant information, retailers build brand loyalty and elevate the shopping experience far beyond a transactional relationship.

Furthermore, the deployment of Natural Language Processing (NLP) enhances these personalized experiences by making interactions feel human and engaging. NLP can extract meaningful insights from customer communications, be it through reviews, chats, or voice interactions. It understands the sentiment and context, allowing brands to fine-tune their responses and content strategy. This level of personalization ensures that customers feel valued and understood, an essential factor in forming enduring relationships with a brand.

Creating such targeted content also has its challenges. Data privacy concerns loom large. Personalization requires access to a plethora of data, sparking conversations about ethical use. Customers are increasingly mindful of how their data is used, and retailers must be transparent in their practices. AI provides tools to anonymize and aggregate data, yet the responsibility to protect consumer privacy and gain their trust remains squarely on the shoulders of businesses.

A practical application of AI in personalized content is the dynamic adjustment of website content. For instance, a returning visitor might see a homepage featuring popular products in their preferred categories, while a first-time shopper might experience a more general promotional message. Even the sequence of product listings can be altered based on predicted preferences, ensuring that each interaction feels customized.

Offline, these digital strategies can be mirrored through smart store technologies. In-store apps can notify employees of a customer's preferences as they enter, so they can offer personalized assistance. Digital signage can dynamically adjust its messaging, based on the demographic profile of the observer, creating a deeply immersive shopping journey that feels bespoke.

Importantly, AI-driven personalization isn't just for large retailers. Even smaller businesses can harness AI tools and platforms designed to facilitate personalized content. From email marketing services offering segmentation based on user behavior to CRM systems with built-in AI analytics, the technology is accessible. This democratization of AI ensures that any retailer, regardless of size, can offer personalized experiences, enhancing customer satisfaction and fostering loyalty.

A good strategy for leveraging AI in personalized content requires thoughtful integration with existing marketing and sales operations. Retailers need to assess their current capabilities and identify areas where AI can make the biggest impact. Small, incremental changes can harness AI's power without the need for a complete overhaul of systems. Retailers should focus not only on the technology itself but also on crafting a strategy that truly understands their audience and provides value at every interaction point.

The future of retail will continue to be shaped by AI-driven personalization. As technology evolves, so will the depth of personalization, potentially moving beyond recommendations to anticipate and respond to consumer needs before they're expressed. Imagine virtual fitting rooms that understand style preferences or checkout aisles configured to display items a customer is most likely to impulse buy. As these technologies become more refined, the potential for a streamlined, highly engaging consumer experience grows exponentially.

In conclusion, AI for personalized content is about creating meaningful and relevant interactions between retailers and consumers. It's about understanding, predicting, and responding to individual needs with precision. As AI continues to develop these capabilities, it will reshape the retail landscape, making highly personalized shopping experiences the rule rather than the exception. Embracing AI means not just keeping pace with consumer expectations but setting new standards in personal engagement. For those looking to lead in the retail industry, harnessing AI's potential for personalized content is not just an option—it's an imperative.

Enhancing Retail Marketing with AI

In today's rapidly evolving retail landscape, the old rules of marketing simply don't cut it anymore. AI is stepping in as a powerful ally for marketers who seek to connect with their audiences in ways that were once unimaginable. By leveraging AI's capabilities, retailers can not only enhance their marketing strategies but also fundamentally transform how they engage with consumers. As expectations shift towards hyper-personalization and instant gratification, AI helps retailers meet these demands with remarkable precision and efficiency.

One of the primary ways AI is revolutionizing retail marketing is by enabling personalized content at scale. In a world oversaturated with information, personal relevance becomes critical. AI utilizes customer data to craft tailored marketing messages that resonate on an individual level. This approach not only increases engagement but also fosters loyalty by making consumers feel understood and valued. Whether it's personalized emails based on browsing history or product suggestions tailored to past purchases, AI-driven personalization transforms how consumers interact with brands.

Beyond personalization, AI enhances marketing efforts through advanced data analytics. Retailers are swimming in data—from social media interactions to sales figures—but making sense of it is a monumental task without the right tools. AI breaks down these silos by processing vast amounts of data in real time, offering actionable insights that can shape marketing strategies. By identifying emerging trends and consumer preferences, AI empowers marketers to make informed decisions and steer their campaigns in the right direction.

Creativity in content creation is another area where AI makes a significant impact. Through tools like natural language generation and computer vision, AI supports marketers in producing engaging content faster and more efficiently. AI can write blogs, design ad visuals, or even produce video scripts tailored to capture attention and drive traffic. This not only reduces the workload on creative teams but also ensures consistency across various marketing channels, maintaining a unified brand voice.

Moreover, AI's predictive analytics capabilities offer a glimpse into the future of retail marketing. By analyzing patterns and historical data, AI can forecast consumer behavior and market trends. This foresight is invaluable for designing campaigns that anticipate consumer needs and expectations. It enables marketers to refine their targeting strategies and optimize their marketing spend, ensuring resources are utilized effectively in hitting the desired targets.

In addition to these predictive capabilities, AI plays a crucial role in real-time marketing adjustments. The dynamic nature of consumer behavior means that static marketing strategies can quickly become outdated. AI-driven insights enable marketers to tweak campaigns in real time, making necessary adjustments based on current performance metrics and changes in consumer sentiment. By doing so, retail marketers can maintain relevance and maximize the impact of their promotional efforts.

The integration of AI in marketing also facilitates a more responsive interaction with consumers. Chatbots powered by AI are at the front lines of customer engagement, offering immediate assistance, product recommendations, or information requests. These interactions are more than transactional; they enrich the consumer experience, building a bridge of trust and engagement between the brand and its customers.

Leveraging AI for segmenting audiences is another game-changer. Instead of broad categorizations, AI can examine demographic, psychographic, and behavioral markers to create highly detailed customer profiles. This granular segmentation allows for the creation of targeted marketing campaigns that speak directly to the unique motivations of each consumer segment. Such precision ensures that marketing messages hit the mark, increasing conversion rates and improving ROI.

AI doesn't just enhance the outward-facing aspect of marketing but also optimizes internal processes. Automated systems manage routine tasks, freeing up time for marketers to focus on creative strategy and innovation. AI-driven tools can schedule social media posts, analyze campaign performance, or even monitor brand reputation, managing aspects that once required significant human attention.

The integration of AI into retail marketing doesn't come without its challenges. There's a fine line between helpful personalization and invasive surveillance. Marketers must tread carefully, ensuring they respect consumer privacy while delivering value through AI. Establishing consumer trust is essential, reinforcing the need for ethical AI practices that prioritize transparency and consent.

As we explore the capabilities of AI in retail marketing, it's clear that this technology is not just a tool—it's a strategic partner. For marketers aiming to thrive in the digital age, embracing AI doesn't just provide a competitive edge; it's becoming a necessity. Retailers who harness the power of AI effectively will find themselves at the forefront of their industry, ready to lead the charge into an AI-enhanced future.

In summary, AI's role in enhancing retail marketing is multifaceted, offering personalized content creation, advanced analytics, and responsive consumer engagement. By embracing these capabilities, retailers can not only stay ahead of the curve but redefine what's possible in their marketing efforts. As you continue to explore AI's potential, the opportunities for innovation and growth are boundless, setting the stage for a new era of retail marketing excellence.

Chapter 13:
The Role of AI in E-commerce

As e-commerce surges ahead, AI stands as a transformative force, revolutionizing how online shopping is experienced and executed. By seamlessly integrating algorithms that learn and adapt, e-commerce platforms can now deliver hyper-personalized shopping experiences that cater to individual preferences with uncanny accuracy. These AI-driven systems analyze customer interactions, extracting meaningful insights that help anticipate desires before they're even articulated. Platforms are evolving rapidly, employing AI to assess purchasing behaviors, optimize recommendation engines, and streamline user interfaces, thereby creating an intuitive and engaging shopping journey. Additionally, the scalability and adaptability of AI empower businesses to innovate faster and respond dynamically to market demands, setting the stage for exponential growth. In this landscape, AI is not just a tool but a strategic partner in crafting unfaltering customer loyalty and uninterrupted business evolution.

Streamlining Online Shopping Experiences

In the fast-paced world of e-commerce, artificial intelligence (AI) is increasingly seen as the catalyst revolutionizing the way consumers interact with online stores. As digital marketplaces grow in complexity, the demand for personalized, efficient, and seamless shopping journeys is higher than ever. AI technologies stand at the forefront, providing automated solutions that streamline various facets of online shopping.

First and foremost, AI enhances user experience by providing highly sophisticated recommendation engines. These engines analyze vast amounts of data from past purchases, browsing history, and even time spent on particular products. This analysis allows for precise, tailored suggestions that align perfectly with a shopper's preferences and needs. The result is a level of personalization that transforms the shopping experience from a static, one-size-fits-all approach into a dynamic, customer-centric journey.

Moreover, the integration of AI in e-commerce platforms aids in simplifying search functionalities. Traditional keyword searches often fail to deliver precise results, especially when consumers aren't sure exactly what they are looking for. AI-driven visual and voice search capabilities are turning this problem on its head. By allowing users to input images or voice commands, these technologies can match products more accurately, making the discovery process both intuitive and engaging. Whether someone snaps a photo of a desired outfit seen on the street or asks a virtual assistant for home décor ideas, AI bridges the gap between intent and purchase.

AI's role extends beyond merely improving search and recommendation capabilities. It plays a significant part in optimizing the backend operations of e-commerce sites. One of the major challenges in online retail is ensuring that a smooth and efficient checkout process is in place. Here, AI intervenes to minimize cart abandonment rates. By analyzing user behavior, AI systems predict and address potential bottlenecks in the customer journey before they happen, offering personalized incentives or streamlined steps to encourage completing a purchase.

Security and fraud prevention are another critical area where AI shines. With incidents of online fraud rising, e-commerce platforms must remain vigilant to protect consumer data and transactions. AI algorithms can automatically detect unusual purchase patterns or anomalous behavior, instantly flagging suspicious activities for further review. This real-time surveillance reduces potential fraud and fosters trust among consumers who choose to transact online.

Furthermore, inventory management has become a seamless process, thanks to AI. With predictive analytics, retailers can better anticipate demand and ensure essential products remain in stock. This technology enables e-commerce platforms to automatically manage restocks, thus minimizing the chances of a customer seeing the dreaded "out of stock" message. It also saves human resources by automating parts of the supply chain, thereby reducing operational costs and enhancing efficiency.

Logistics, too, are significantly impacted. AI-driven systems can analyze traffic patterns, predict optimal shipping routes, and ensure timely delivery of goods. This not only optimizes the supply chain management processes but also reduces shipping times, facilitating quicker service to consumers. Faster delivery not only satisfies customer expectations but also gives retailers a competitive edge.

Chatbots are another pivotal AI-driven tool transforming online shopping. They provide 24/7 customer support, answering queries and assisting in the decision-making process, all without human intervention. What's impressive is the continuous learning these bots undergo, adapting to communication styles, and improving the quality of assistance over time. Shoppers can get instant support, product recommendations, and even style suggestions tailored to their taste, enhancing their overall shopping experience.

Take, for example, the application of AI in managing and curating content. Through machine learning algorithms, e-commerce sites can analyze consumer interactions and preferences to generate personalized content sequences. These might include emails, notifications, and special promotions tailored specifically to individual tastes and historical data. This type of engagement not only retains customers but also drives further sales by keeping brands at the forefront of shoppers' minds.

The convergence of AI with augmented reality (AR) marks a significant milestone in online shopping, providing an immersive experience that bridges the gap between the online and physical worlds. Shoppers often hesitate before making a purchase because they can't interact with the product physically. AR, powered by AI, can project digital images onto the real world, allowing consumers to visualize how products might look in their space or worn on their bodies. This feature minimizes returns and increases customer satisfaction as buyers feel more confident in their purchasing decision.

In the field of dynamic pricing, AI has reshaped competitive strategies. It allows retailers to adjust prices in real-time based on machine learning insights into market demand, competitor pricing, and consumer purchasing patterns. This intelligence enables businesses to maximize profits while maintaining a competitive stance in ever-fluctuating markets.

These technological advancements, powered by AI, streamline online shopping by removing friction points and crafting a more personalized and engaging shopping journey. The combination of ease, security, and personalization that AI delivers not only contributes to improved customer satisfaction but also fosters brand loyalty and drives growth in the e-commerce domain. As AI continues to evolve, online retailers who leverage these tools will be well-positioned to meet and exceed the expectations of modern consumers.

This revolution in e-commerce doesn't mean challenges aren't present. Ethical considerations and data privacy remain persistent issues. As AI systems capture and process consumer data to create tailored experiences, maintaining transparency and trust becomes crucial. Retailers must commit to ethical AI practices that respect user privacy and adhere to legal standards to secure consumer trust and loyalty in an AI-driven marketplace.

In conclusion, AI is a transformative force in streamlining online shopping experiences, providing tools that make the shopping journey intuitive, secure, and gratifying. While challenges remain, the limitless potential of AI in e-commerce promises not only to reshape retail but also to mold the future of how we shop. Retailers embracing this technology will find themselves at the pinnacle of innovation, set on forging new paths in the digital shopping landscape.

AI-Driven Platforms for E-commerce Growth

In the rapidly evolving world of e-commerce, AI-driven platforms have become instrumental in reshaping how businesses operate and interact with customers. These platforms leverage the power of artificial intelligence to enhance decision-making, streamline operations, and create personalized shopping experiences. The traditional e-commerce model, which once relied heavily on manual processing and human intuition, is now increasingly being augmented by AI technologies that drive efficiency, accuracy, and scalability. Through intelligent automation and data-driven insights, businesses can stay competitive in a fast-paced digital marketplace.

One of the most significant impacts of AI-driven platforms in e-commerce is on personalization. By analyzing vast amounts of data, AI can identify individual consumer preferences and behaviors, enabling businesses to provide personalized recommendations and targeted marketing. This level of customization not only enhances the customer experience but also increases conversion rates as consumers are more likely to engage with products and offers that resonate with them. With AI, marketers are empowered to deliver precision-targeted content that feels bespoke, making the whole shopping experience seamlessly tailored to each consumer.

A key component of these platforms is their ability to process and analyze big data in real time. This capability allows retailers to adapt quickly to market changes and consumer trends, ensuring that their strategies are always aligned with current demands. For example, AI-driven analytics tools can predict which products are likely to be in demand and when, guiding inventory management decisions and preventing stockouts or overstock situations. This kind of agility is crucial in maintaining customer satisfaction and fostering loyalty.

Moreover, AI platforms are transforming the logistics and supply chain segments of e-commerce businesses. Complex algorithms can optimize delivery routes, reduce shipping times, and lower costs, ultimately improving the overall efficiency of the supply chain. Predictive maintenance powered by AI can also foresee equipment failures before they occur, reducing downtime and maintaining a smooth operational flow. Such innovations are crucial in an era where quick and reliable delivery is not just an expectation but a necessity for competing in the digital commerce arena.

AI-driven platforms provide businesses with powerful tools for dynamic pricing strategies, allowing them to adjust prices in real time based on factors such as demand, competition, and customer preferences. This approach ensures that prices are competitive while maximizing profits. For many businesses, this capability has been game-changing, as it allows them to respond instantly to market fluctuations and consumer behavior changes. This level of flexibility is only possible with the advanced analytical capabilities provided by AI systems.

Another critical area where AI platforms shine is in customer service. By implementing AI-powered chatbots and virtual assistants, e-commerce businesses can offer 24/7 customer support, addressing queries and providing assistance even outside normal business hours. These AI tools are constantly learning and improving, ensuring that they can provide accurate and timely responses as they gather more interaction data. As a result, businesses can handle larger volumes of inquiries with consistent quality, ultimately enhancing the overall customer experience.

The integration of AI-driven platforms with visual recognition technology also facilitates an innovative approach to e-commerce. With AI, image recognition can be utilized for visual search capabilities, enabling users to search for products using images instead of text. This not only simplifies the search process but also aligns with the growing consumer preference for visual content. As image-based search and shopping become more prevalent, AI technology will become even more essential for e-commerce platforms looking to capitalize on these trends.

AI-driven e-commerce platforms aren't just limited to enhancing current operations; they are also pivotal in driving future innovations. By continuously analyzing customer feedback and market data, these platforms can identify trends and opportunities that inform future developments and product offerings. As AI technologies continue to evolve, they promise to unlock even more avenues for growth and innovation in e-commerce, shaping an increasingly automated and intelligent retail landscape.

In summary, AI-driven platforms are at the heart of the transformation within the e-commerce sector. They empower businesses with the tools needed to deliver personalized shopping experiences, optimize operations, and adapt to changing markets swiftly. As AI continues to advance, these platforms will undoubtedly become even more sophisticated, offering new possibilities and uncovering new paths for growth. E-commerce businesses willing to embrace these technologies will be better positioned to capitalize on the benefits of AI, ensuring their sustained success in an increasingly competitive environment.

Chapter 14:
Workforce Transformation in Retail

The retail industry's workforce is undergoing a profound transformation driven by AI, reshaping roles and redefining skills in an era of technological advancement. As automation takes over routine tasks, employees find themselves transitioning towards more strategic positions that harness human creativity and emotional intelligence. New roles are emerging, such as AI trainers and data analysts, requiring workers to embrace continuous learning and adaptability. This shift is not just about replacing jobs but augmenting human capabilities, creating a collaborative environment where technology and staff work hand-in-hand to enhance customer experiences. Retailers who invest in upskilling their workforce are likely to thrive, turning challenges into opportunities and forging a more resilient future. The focus lies in nurturing a workforce that's not only tech-savvy but also capable of leveraging AI-driven insights to drive innovation and growth in a rapidly changing market.

AI's Impact on Retail Jobs

We're living in an era where artificial intelligence is rapidly reshaping industries, and retail is no exception. AI's impact on retail jobs is profound, and it's driving a workforce transformation that's both exciting and challenging. The advent of AI technologies in retail is akin to the industrial revolutions of the past—where automation and innovation disrupted traditional roles. Yet, it's a double-edged sword, bringing both opportunities and challenges.

Historically, new technologies have altered the labor market landscape, and AI is doing just that. In many retail spaces, AI is taking over routine and repetitive tasks. For example, automated checkout systems and inventory robots have decreased the need for manual labor in these areas. It's not just about replacing jobs, though; AI is streamlining processes to ensure that human employees can focus on tasks that require creativity and complex decision-making.

The role of the retail employee is evolving. As AI handles more back-end operations, employees are being shifted to front-of-house responsibilities. These include enhancing customer engagement and delivering personalized shopping experiences, tasks that AI supports but humans still excel at. This transition signifies a shift in the necessary skill set for retail workers, prompting a focus on soft skills like communication and emotional intelligence.

Moreover, AI isn't just about streamlining operations—it's about innovation and creating new roles altogether. Retailers are increasingly seeking data analysts, AI specialists, and tech-savvy managers to navigate this brave new world. For those in the industry willing to adapt, there's a wealth of opportunity for learning and career expansion. As AI continues to develop, so too will the ways in which humans harness its potential.

However, this transformation doesn't come without its challenges. One of the primary concerns is job displacement. Many worry that automation will lead to significant layoffs. It's critical for organizations to address these concerns by providing workforce training and development opportunities. Equipping workers with the necessary skills to transition into new roles is not just beneficial for individuals but essential for business success.

Education systems also have a role to play. Developing curricula that integrate technology and innovation management can prepare upcoming generations for the changing job market. Partnerships between educational institutions and retail companies can facilitate hands-on learning experiences, helping mitigate the skills gap that AI might create.

The impact of AI doesn't occur in a vacuum. Retail jobs are also being influenced by global economic shifts, demographic changes, and consumer preferences. It's imperative for retailers to keep these factors in mind while planning for workforce changes. A dynamic and holistic approach will be crucial in navigating these uncharted waters.

While some see AI as a threat to retail jobs, others view it as an enhancement tool. Intelligent systems can assist employees by providing real-time insights and recommendations, making them more efficient and empowering them to perform at their best. For example, AI-driven analytics tools can help sales associates understand customer preferences and suggest appropriate products, thereby improving customer satisfaction and loyalty.

Creating strategic frameworks to integrate AI with human resources will be key to unlocking its full potential. Organizations that can adeptly balance AI-powered automation with human creativity and insight will find themselves leading the pack. Emphasizing collaborative AI-human environments can result in a more engaged and motivated workforce, leading to true innovation in retail.

As we continue to see AI's footprint expand in the retail sector, companies need to foster a culture of continuous learning. Encouraging employees to embrace technology-driven changes can make them feel invested in their roles and future careers. Encouragingly, many retailers are already taking steps to train their workforce and cultivate an adaptable and forward-thinking culture.

AI is also catalyzing a change in how retail employees perceive their work. No longer just about selling products, retail roles are increasingly about creating experiences and building relationships. This shift not only appeals to consumers but makes the work more fulfilling for employees, potentially leading to a deeper commitment to their roles.

In conclusion, while AI ushers in new challenges, it also opens doors to endless possibilities. The workforce transformation in retail is about leveraging AI to enhance human capabilities, not replace them. The future of retail jobs lies in a collaborative approach where technology and human skills coexist, creating a dynamic industry poised for innovation and growth.

Embracing New Skills and Roles

The retail industry, ever dynamic, finds itself at the intersection of technology and talent as AI shapes its future. As artificial intelligence becomes deeply embedded in the fabric of retail operations, the need for the workforce to adapt has never been more pressing. The days of traditional retail roles are evolving, giving rise to new skill sets and job descriptions that marry technology with human intuition.

In the past, retail workers often relied on instinct and experience to make decisions. Now, AI empowers them with data-driven insights, transforming how decisions are made. This shift doesn't negate the need for human touch but emphasizes the need for workers who can interpret data, understand AI outputs, and apply these insights effectively. Retail employees must transition into roles that require analytical and technical skills while retaining their ability to connect with customers.

This transformation journey for the workforce isn't merely about training employees on how to use AI tools. It's about fostering a mindset that embraces continual learning and adaptability. Reskilling and upskilling initiatives are crucial in this regard, as they equip employees with the necessary competencies to thrive in an AI-enhanced environment. Workshops, seminars, and online courses have become instrumental for retailers intent on smoothing this transition.

Moreover, the integration of AI has spurred the creation of entirely new roles that didn't exist a decade ago. Jobs such as AI trainers, data analysts, and machine-learning specialists are becoming commonplace. These roles not only reflect the need to manage AI tools but also underscore the importance of individuals who can bridge the gap between technology and retail operations.

Retailers are recognizing the value of these new roles and are investing heavily in their formation. By cultivating a workforce proficient in AI and data analytics, businesses can ensure they remain competitive. This initiative also empowers employees, providing them with growth opportunities that align with industry trends.

The impact of this transformation is visible across various segments of the retail sector. For example, in customer service, traditional roles are shifting towards more complex problem-solving tasks as AI handles routine inquiries. Employees are becoming orchestrators of superior customer experiences, leveraging AI insights to personalize interactions and anticipate customer needs.

Similarly, in supply chain management, AI plays a pivotal role in optimizing processes and forecasting demand. Here, the workforce is adapting by learning how to work alongside these systems, interpreting AI-generated recommendations to streamline logistics and enhance efficiency.

As AI continues to redefine job descriptions, the importance of soft skills remains undiminished. In fact, skills such as communication, empathy, and problem-solving are more critical now than ever. They complement technical abilities and ensure that technology serves people, not the other way around. Retail leaders must nurture these soft skills, ensuring a balanced approach where technology and human elements coalesce seamlessly.

Retailers are not alone in this endeavor. Partnerships with educational institutions and technology providers are emerging as a viable strategy for developing the skills needed in this new era. These collaborations help create curricula that accurately reflect industry needs, ensuring that training programs resonate with real-world applications.

With AI's role steadily increasing, some might fear that automation could lead to job losses. However, the current trajectory in the retail landscape suggests a blend of AI augmentation and human creativity. AI takes over repetitive tasks, thus freeing up employees to focus on more meaningful work that machines can't perform. The result is a more engaged and innovative workforce.

Retailers embracing these changes are setting a precedent, demonstrating that AI can enrich human roles rather than replace them. Through this lens, AI appears less as a threat and more as a tool for empowerment, providing the workforce with new ways to deliver value and craft exceptional shopping experiences.

In conclusion, embracing new skills and roles in retail is about more than mere adaptation; it's about capitalizing on the opportunities AI presents to redefine work, drive innovation, and foster growth. As the industry continues to evolve, retail professionals at all levels must remain agile, visionary, and ready to embrace change as they navigate this new landscape.

Chapter 15:
Retail Analytics and Insights

As we navigate the transformative landscape of AI in retail, the power of retail analytics and insights becomes undeniably crucial. Today, businesses harness vast amounts of big data to decode complex consumer behaviors and preferences, ultimately shaping strategic decisions that drive success. AI-driven tools offer retailers unprecedented intelligence, enabling them to predict trends, optimize operations, and enhance customer experiences like never before. These insights are not just numbers; they're the narrative of consumer engagement and market dynamics. Retailers equipped with these advanced analytical capabilities can swiftly adapt to market changes, remain competitive, and foster innovation within their organization. The era of relying solely on intuition is fading—real-time, data-backed insights are now the cornerstone of strategic planning and execution. By seamlessly integrating AI with retail operations, organizations turn data into actionable intelligence, driving growth and setting the stage for a future where foresight is the new currency. In this chapter, we delve into the revolutionary impact of analytics and uncover how leveraging AI tools is essential for thriving in the modern retail environment.

Leveraging Big Data for Retail Success

In the ever-evolving landscape of retail, the ability to harness and utilize big data effectively can be the differentiator between thriving and merely surviving. The influx of vast amounts of data, ranging from transaction logs to social media interactions, has opened a new horizon of opportunities for retailers. Big data isn't just a buzzword; it is the backbone of modern retail analytics and insights. By leveraging big data, retailers can offer personalized shopping experiences, optimize inventory, enhance customer service, and ultimately drive profitability. The potential is vast and the early adopters are already reaping substantial rewards.

At the heart of big data's impact on retail lies the ability to understand customers at a granular level. Traditionally, retailers relied on broad demographic data to segment their audience. Now, with data pouring in from multiple touchpoints, each customer can be seen as a unique individual. This detail level enables highly personalized marketing strategies, targeting customers with precisely what they want, when they want it. This personalization is not just about boosting sales; it enhances customer satisfaction and loyalty, which are paramount in today's competitive market. Moreover, by analyzing shopping patterns and preferences, retailers can anticipate needs and create proactive solutions.

The transformation extends to inventory management, an area where big data's contributions are incredibly tangible. By analyzing historical sales data, weather patterns, social media signals, and even local events, businesses can predict demand with unprecedented accuracy. This foresight allows for just-in-time inventory systems, reducing costs tied up in unsold goods and minimizing waste. Efficient inventory management not only improves a retailer's bottom line but also contributes to sustainability goals, as overproduction and overstocking are significant concerns in the retail world.

Big data also empowers retailers with real-time insights into their operations. Through data analytics dashboards, companies can monitor sales performance, inventory levels, and supply chain efficiencies, making informed decisions swiftly. These insights are invaluable in an industry where margins are often slim, and any inefficiencies can have a costly toll. By continuously analyzing operational data, retailers can identify bottlenecks, optimize processes, and enhance customer satisfaction, driving long-term growth and success.

However, leveraging big data is not without its challenges. Data collection, management, and analysis require sophisticated tools and a skilled workforce. Retailers must invest in advanced analytics platforms capable of processing and interpreting vast datasets. Furthermore, there is the critical aspect of data privacy and security. Customers are increasingly aware of their data rights, and any breach or misuse can seriously damage a brand's reputation. Retailers must ensure compliance with legal standards and ethical practices to maintain consumer trust.

Beyond customer analytics and operational improvements, big data has transformative potential in shaping the future of retail innovation. For example, retailers can utilize big data to experiment with dynamic pricing strategies, adjusting prices in real time based on supply, demand, and competitor pricing. This real-time responsiveness can enhance competitiveness and profitability, offering a significant edge over slower-reacting competitors.

The integration of big data into retail frameworks provides a detailed map for retailers looking to expand their market reach. By analyzing consumer behaviors across different regions, retailers can tailor their strategies to fit local preferences and norms. This adaptability is crucial in a globalized market where cultural nuances significantly influence purchasing decisions. Furthermore, insights gained from big data analytics can guide strategic decisions regarding store placements, promotional campaigns, and product availability tailored to specific geographical locations.

While the potential of big data analytics is vast, retailers must strategically approach its implementation. It's essential to define clear objectives and KPIs to measure the success of big data initiatives. Retailers should start with small, manageable projects before scaling up, using initial successes as a foundation for broader implementations. By integrating big data initiatives with overall business strategies, retailers can ensure that insights are actionable and benefits are tangible.

In conclusion, leveraging big data for retail success is not a future possibility—it's a present-day necessity. The insights garnered from robust data analytics can inform every aspect of a retail business, from understanding individual customers to optimizing global supply chains. As retailers continue to navigate the data-driven landscape, those who effectively harness the power of big data will lead the charge toward innovation and sustainability in the retail sector. Embracing this paradigm shift is less about following a trend and more about staying relevant and competitive in an increasingly digital world.

AI Tools for Retail Intelligence

In the bustling world of retail, where competition is fierce and consumer preferences seem to shift with the winds, retailers need more than just gut feeling and intuition to thrive. This is where AI tools for retail intelligence come into play. They're transforming the way businesses gather, analyze, and leverage data, providing insights that are crucial for making informed decisions and staying ahead in the market.

At the heart of AI-powered retail intelligence is the ability to churn through vast amounts of data swiftly and accurately. Unlike traditional business intelligence tools that might struggle with unstructured data, AI systems excel in processing diverse data types ranging from customer feedback and social media chatter to in-store behavior and transaction history. With this capability, retailers gain a comprehensive view of their operations, customer preferences, and the overall market landscape. In essence, AI turns a haystack of data into valuable needles of information.

Predictive analytics, a key component of AI in retail intelligence, offers a way to forecast future trends by analyzing past patterns. For instance, by examining historical sales data alongside current market conditions and consumer behavior, AI can predict which products will be in demand during particular seasons or events. This allows retailers to optimize their inventory ahead of time, reducing the risk of stockouts or overstocking, which directly impacts their bottom line.

Furthermore, AI tools help retailers understand consumer sentiment like never before. By employing natural language processing (NLP) and sentiment analysis, AI can decipher customer sentiments expressed in product reviews, social media posts, and customer service interactions. These insights are invaluable for tailoring marketing strategies, improving product offerings, and enhancing customer experience.

A powerful aspect of AI in retail intelligence is competitor analysis. AI tools can monitor competitors' pricing strategies, promotional activities, and even their customer feedback. With machine learning algorithms, retailers can uncover these patterns and devise strategies to address gaps or capitalize on opportunities. This level of insight is crucial in devising competitive pricing strategies and understanding market positioning.

Moreover, AI is redefining how retailers engage with local markets by enabling hyper-local insights. By analyzing demographic data, local market trends, and cultural preferences, AI assists retailers in tailoring their offerings to specific geographic areas. This localization can boost engagement and sales significantly, as customers feel that products and marketing are speaking directly to their needs and preferences.

Retailers are also leveraging AI tools to optimize their supply chain operations, which in turn influences retail intelligence. With intelligent supply chain management, retailers can map the journey of goods from production to the consumer, flagging inefficiencies or potential disruptions before they impact the business. This proactive approach is part of a broader strategy where insight gained from AI leads to a seamless and responsive supply chain.

Collaborative filtering and recommendation systems powered by AI have been game-changers in personalizing customer shopping experiences, but they also provide another layer of intelligence for retailers. By analyzing which products are often bought together or what customers with similar shopping patterns purchase, retailers can better manage inventory and suggest effective bundling strategies.

In the age of big data, AI tools for retail intelligence don't just stop at data collection and analysis. Visualization tools powered by AI turn complex data sets into easy-to-understand, actionable insights. Interactive dashboards provide retailers with real-time data visualization, helping them quickly identify trends, track KPIs, and make timely decisions.

AI's immersion into retail doesn't stop at generating insights—it extends into streamlining communication across departments. With AI-driven insights, product development, marketing, and sales teams can align their strategies, leading to a cohesive approach that reflects the entire business's goals and insights.

The journey toward embracing AI tools for retail intelligence is not devoid of challenges. Companies must consider data privacy and security, ensuring that consumer data is handled with the utmost care and that insights are derived ethically. Moreover, integrating AI systems requires an initial investment in time and resources. Training the workforce to interpret and act on AI-generated insights is crucial for maximizing these technologies' potential.

Ultimately, AI-powered retail intelligence equips retailers with the tools needed to adapt and thrive in an ever-changing landscape. It allows them to be agile, proactive, and customer-centric, arming them with insights that are not just about surviving but excelling in a competitive market. As AI continues to evolve, its role in retail will only deepen, promising even greater precision and enhanced capabilities in decision-making and strategy development.

Chapter 16:
AI in Fashion Retail

Within the vivid and ever-evolving realm of fashion, AI emerges as a trailblazer, transforming the industry with an unparalleled blend of creativity and analytics. This digital revolution allows retailers to predict trends through sophisticated algorithms, turning historical data and market demand into fashion-forward designs that resonate with consumers. AI's influence extends beyond design into the shopping experience itself, offering virtual fitting rooms and personalized recommendations that echo a shopper's unique style. By analyzing customer preferences and behaviors, AI enriches every stage of the fashion journey, ensuring that retailers meet and exceed evolving consumer expectations. The integration of AI empowers brands not only to streamline operations but also to cultivate deeper relationships with their consumers, capturing the art of fashion with the precision of cutting-edge technology. As AI continues to weave itself into the fabric of fashion retail, it unveils a future where innovation and intuition harmoniously redefine the style narrative.

Predictive Modeling in Design

Stepping into the future of fashion retail, we encounter the transformative power of predictive modeling in design. This pivotal technology leverages vast amounts of data to anticipate trends, predict consumer preferences, and drive creativity, fundamentally altering the design process. As AI integrates deeper into the realm of fashion, predictive modeling stands as a critical tool for designers, allowing them to create collections that align with both current market demands and future trends.

Predictive modeling utilizes data from a multitude of sources, including social media trends, sales figures, and consumer feedback, to generate insights. These insights help designers understand emerging patterns and forecast what consumers will desire. This capability not only enhances design accuracy but also reduces waste by limiting overproduction and aligning inventory more closely with consumer demand.

One fascinating aspect of predictive modeling is its ability to identify micro-trends, which can be fleeting and difficult to catch through traditional analysis. AI can sift through massive datasets with speed and precision, uncovering these subtle trends and giving designers the edge in a highly competitive market. For fast fashion brands, this means they can respond to new trends almost immediately, ensuring they always offer the latest styles.

Predictive modeling also empowers designers to experiment with new materials and styles while still staying within the bounds of consumer interest. By predicting which fabrics, patterns, and colors will be popular, AI can guide designers in their creative processes, allowing for innovation that is rooted in data-driven insights. This blend of creativity and technology fosters a more sustainable approach to fashion design, as it minimizes the risk of producing collections that don't sell.

Moreover, predictive modeling isn't just about forecasting what will sell; it's also about understanding how various styles and designs resonate with different demographic groups. By analyzing consumer data, AI helps brands personalize their offerings, tailoring designs to meet the specific tastes and preferences of diverse customer segments. This level of personalization enables brands to create more inclusive collections that appeal to a broader audience, enhancing brand loyalty and customer satisfaction.

In addition to tailoring designs, predictive modeling aids in strategic planning by forecasting sales volumes for upcoming seasons. This allows brands to optimize their production schedules and allocate resources more efficiently. By anticipating demand more accurately, they can reduce excess inventory and logistical costs, improving profitability while contributing to a sustainable retail model.

Interestingly, predictive modeling can even predict geographical variations in fashion trends. What might be popular in urban centers could differ significantly from trends in suburban or rural areas. By identifying these regional differences, fashion brands can tailor their marketing and distribution strategies accordingly, ensuring that the right products reach the right markets.

The impact of AI's predictive models extends further into enhancing collaborations with manufacturers. By providing accurate forecasts and design specifications, fashion brands can work more efficiently with their supply chain partners. This synchronization reduces lead times and ensures that designs move from conception to shelf with minimal delays.

One transformative example of predictive modeling in fashion retail is its role in sustainable practices. By accurately predicting demand, brands can focus on producing what is necessary, thus avoiding the environmental repercussions of overproduction. This aligns closely with the growing consumer demand for eco-friendly and sustainable fashion choices.

Furthermore, predictive modeling can help brands navigate economic challenges by anticipating shifts in consumer spending. During economic downturns or shifts in consumer priorities, understanding which product categories might remain resilient can help brands make informed decisions about where to focus their design efforts and marketing budgets.

AI's role in predictive modeling also offers the potential for a more democratized fashion industry. Aspiring designers can access data-driven insights that were once only available to large brands with substantial resources. This opens doors for new talent to understand market demands and bring innovative designs to life, leveling the playing field and encouraging a greater diversity of fashion voices.

Ultimately, predictive modeling in design represents a fusion of art and science. By aligning creativity with data-driven insights, fashion retailers are not only revolutionizing the design process but also enhancing their strategic capabilities. This synergy allows them to remain agile in a rapidly changing market, anticipate consumer needs, and deliver products that resonate with their audience.

As the fashion industry continues to embrace AI-driven technologies, predictive modeling will further evolve, incorporating more complex algorithms and a broader array of data sources. The future of fashion will likely see even more integrated and sophisticated models, enabling brands to not only predict but also influence fashion trends. By leading the way in innovation, predictive modeling is poised to drive the fashion industry forward, transforming challenges into opportunities for growth and creativity.

Enhancing the Shopping Experience

In the ever-evolving landscape of fashion retail, enhancing the shopping experience with AI is a transformative force. Traditionally, shopping was a sensory voyage where textiles were touched, garments tried on, and in-store interactions shaped our decisions. However, AI has introduced a new paradigm, one that's redefining these experiences beyond physical boundaries. By seamlessly integrating AI into retail operations, the fashion industry is poised to cater to the nuanced expectations of modern consumers.

Personalization is at the heart of this transformation. AI algorithms analyze vast amounts of data—from purchase histories and browsing patterns to social media behavior—to create deeply personalized shopping experiences. Imagine walking into a store or landing on an online platform that already knows your preferences. Recommendations are no longer generic; they're tailor-made. This degree of customization not only enhances customer satisfaction but also drives engagement, making shopping a more meaningful and gratifying endeavor.

Virtual fitting rooms are a compelling development. AI-powered virtual try-on technologies allow customers to visualize how clothes fit and look without physically trying them on. By using augmented reality and sophisticated image processing, shoppers can examine outfits from every angle with just a few swipes on their devices. This innovation significantly reduces return rates, a long-standing challenge for online retailers, and offers consumers the confidence to make purchases unseen, expanding the boundaries of retail reach.

AI's role in enhancing the shopping experience is not limited to the visual and personal. It extends to anticipatory service offerings. Predictive analytics use AI to anticipate consumer needs, suggesting complementary products, notifying customers of restocks, or even alerting them to promotions they're likely to be interested in. These predictive capabilities transform the retail model from reactive to proactive, further cementing consumer loyalty and satisfaction.

Moreover, AI systems are increasingly being leveraged to streamline customer interactions. Chatbots, now more intuitive than ever, serve as personal shopping assistants available 24/7. Beyond simple question-answer protocols, these AI-driven chatbots can handle complex inquiries, provide product recommendations, and assist in purchase decisions, all while maintaining a friendly and conversational tone. Such efficiency in handling customer queries not only enhances the shopping experience but also builds a brand's reputation for excellent service.

However, enhancing the shopping experience with AI is not just about more engaging and efficient sales processes. It's equally about the richness of insights that AI provides to the retailer. Understanding customer behavior at a granular level—how they interact with products, what influences their choices, where they face hurdles— enables retailers to fine-tune their strategies and ultimately offer better shopping experiences.

AI is also transforming how stores operate in physical spaces through the use of smart mirrors and intelligent displays. These technologies can recognize individual customers and provide tailored outfit suggestions, styling tips, or upsell opportunities, blending the convenience of online shopping with the tactile pleasure of in-store experiences. Retailers can adjust in real-time to customer preferences, dynamically reflecting inventory updates or recent trends.

The integration of AI in fashion retail extends beyond the consumer-facing side; it impacts the backend significantly as well. Technologies like AI-driven logistics and inventory management systems ensure that products are available where and when they're most needed, minimizing stockouts and optimizing storage. This operational efficiency not only enhances shopping experiences by ensuring availability but also maximizes profitability by reducing unnecessary surplus.

As AI continues to evolve, ethical considerations in designing these enhanced experiences become paramount. AI's ability to collect and process personal data presents privacy concerns that retailers must navigate sensitively. Ensuring data protection and transparency is crucial to maintaining consumer trust, which in turn embodies the very essence of a positive shopping experience.

The potential of AI to enhance the shopping experience in fashion retail is vast and largely untapped. As AI technologies grow more sophisticated, they promise to make shopping more intuitive, personalized, and enjoyable—a win-win for both retailers and consumers. In embracing these technologies, the industry does not just adopt new tools but embarks on a journey towards a future where shopping is seamlessly integrated into everyday life, adapting swiftly to each individual's style and needs.

Ultimately, the integration of AI in fashion retail is a tale of augmentation rather than replacement. It's about enhancing human creativity and consumer satisfaction with the power of intelligent technology, making the shopping experience not only more efficient but also more exhilarating. By continuously refining these systems, fashion retailers are not just keeping up with modern expectations; they are setting new standards for what it means to shop in the digital age.

Chapter 17:
Sustainability and AI

In the evolving landscape of retail, sustainability has emerged as a critical priority, and AI is playing a transformative role in achieving this vision. By harnessing the power of AI, retailers can significantly minimize waste through optimized inventory management and demand forecasting, ensuring that products are produced and distributed efficiently. Artificial intelligence shines a light on supply chain inefficiencies, enabling a shift towards more sustainable practices that reduce environmental impact. From refining logistics to pinpointing sustainability hotspots across the operational spectrum, AI offers actionable insights that help businesses make data-driven decisions in their pursuit of sustainability. In essence, AI is not just streamlining operations but also fostering a future where profitability and environmental stewardship go hand in hand, inspiring a new era of responsible commerce that resonates with eco-conscious consumers and forward-thinking enterprises alike.

Reducing Waste with AI Solutions

Sustainability isn't just a buzzword; it's become a critical mission for many businesses, particularly in the retail sector. With AI stepping into the picture, companies are discovering powerful ways to cut waste, whether it's through smarter inventory management, optimized logistics, or reducing the carbon footprint associated with retail operations. AI's potential to minimize waste paves the way for more sustainable practices, fundamentally changing how resources are utilized.

One of the most significant areas where AI is making a difference is inventory management. By employing AI-driven algorithms, retailers can more accurately predict customer demand. This predictive capability allows them to stock only what is needed, substantially reducing surplus inventory that often ends up in landfills. Traditional methods of inventory prediction fell short due to their reliance on historical data and static forecasting models. AI, however, can analyze real-time data and adjust stock levels dynamically, ensuring that products are available when needed and reducing the likelihood of overproduction.

Logistics is another frontier where AI is combating waste. The transportation and distribution of goods contribute significantly to the carbon footprint of retail operations. AI can optimize delivery routes and streamline supply chains, leading to reduced fuel consumption and fewer emissions. Through machine learning models, delivery schedules are adjusted dynamically based on factors like weather conditions, traffic patterns, and haul capacity. This not only minimizes environmental impact but also reduces operational costs, creating a dual benefit for both the planet and the bottom line.

Consider the impact of AI in waste reduction within the fashion industry—a notorious contributor to environmental pollution. Fast fashion's rise has led to excessive waste, but AI can help brands predict fashion trends and consumer preferences with remarkable precision. By knowing what will be in demand, retailers can adjust production volumes, lowering the instances of unsold stock that are eventually discarded. Moreover, AI can support circular economy models by assisting in the retrieval and recycling of fashion items, further closing the loop on waste generation.

AI's role in reducing waste extends beyond just physical goods; it also addresses energy consumption. Smart systems powered by AI can manage energy use in retail spaces, determining when to lower heating, adjust lighting, or turn off power to unused areas. Such systems analyze data to make real-time decisions that prevent energy waste, often a major operational cost in large retail environments. This contributes not only to sustainability goals but also significantly impacts cost savings over time.

The reduction of waste is also about improving end-of-life processes for products. AI can contribute through advanced sorting systems that intelligently separate recyclables from waste. Retailers can incorporate AI to enhance their recycling processes, automating what was traditionally a labor-intensive activity. By doing so, they increase recycling rates and decrease the volume of waste sent to landfills. This technological incorporation into waste management shows how AI supports a broader sustainability strategy.

Packaging is another area ripe for AI-driven innovation. Retailers, particularly those transitioning to more eco-friendly practices, face the challenge of balancing protective packaging with environmental impact. AI can optimize packaging solutions by predicting the exact amount of material needed to safely ship products, thus minimizing excess packing materials. Furthermore, AI can design materials that are more recyclable or biodegradable, reducing the environmental toll of packaging waste.

The intersection of AI and sustainability in retail isn't merely a technological or environmental issue—it's a transformative business strategy. With consumers increasingly valuing sustainability, retailers adopting AI solutions to reduce waste can differentiate themselves in a competitive market. This not only attracts eco-conscious customers but also aligns businesses with regulatory standards that are becoming more stringent concerning environmental impact.

AI's solutions span not just the physical aspects of retail but extend into consumer engagement strategies as well. By analyzing consumer feedback, AI can help retailers design products that better meet consumer needs, thereby reducing returns and the associated waste. Returns represent a significant portion of waste in retail; products are returned, processed, and often disposed of rather than resold. Improving product design with AI insights helps create more satisfying consumer experiences and reduces the volume of returns.

Despite the clear advantages, the integration of AI in waste reduction isn't without challenges. Retailers must navigate the technological complexity and ensure that their data systems are capable of supporting advanced AI programs. Furthermore, there's a need for collaboration across industries to develop the standards and infrastructures that will make such AI applications universally beneficial.

Moving forward, the focus should be on innovation while learning from existing deployments. Success stories in AI-waste reduction illustrate the long-term potential of these technologies. Companies that have successfully integrated AI into their sustainability practices often report not just environmental savings, but significant cost efficiencies and enhanced brand loyalty.

Overall, AI provides a compelling suite of solutions that, if implemented thoughtfully, can drastically reduce waste in retail operations. This transformation necessitates a paradigm shift in how businesses think about sustainability—not merely as compliance but as an opportunity for ingenuity and growth. As AI technologies continue to evolve, so will their capabilities to drive sustainable practices, reshaping the industry's future and leaving a positive impact on the planet.

AI's Role in Sustainable Retail Practices

In the rapidly evolving landscape of retail, sustainability is becoming not just a buzzword but a core aspect of business strategy. The integration of AI in sustainable retail practices offers a revolutionary approach that aligns economic benefits with environmental consciousness. By leveraging AI, retailers are now uniquely positioned to foster sustainable solutions that resonate with both consumer values and global environmental goals.

One of the key contributions of AI to sustainable retail practices is its capability in optimizing supply chains. Traditional supply chains often struggle with inefficiencies that result in excess waste and increased carbon emissions. AI's predictive analytics can streamline these processes by predicting demand more accurately, reducing overproduction, and minimizing unnecessary stockpile. For instance, by analyzing historical sales data and real-time market trends, AI systems can forecast product demand with high precision, enabling retailers to adjust their inventory accordingly.

AI is also making headway in reducing energy consumption within retail operations. Smart grids and AI-driven energy management systems help retailers monitor and control their energy usage. This is achieved by integrating AI into heating, ventilation, and air conditioning systems, turning them into intelligent systems that adapt to the number of people in a store and external weather conditions, therefore, ensuring energy is not wasted.

Furthermore, AI technologies are instrumental in developing sustainable packaging solutions. Retailers are increasingly turning to AI-driven design processes to create packaging that is not only more eco-friendly but also maintains product integrity. By simulating the stress and strain on different packaging materials, AI can recommend the optimal design and materials that reduce the environmental impact and lower transportation costs.

The role of AI in sustainable fashion retail is particularly noteworthy. The fashion industry has long been criticized for its environmental impact, but with AI, retailers can adopt more sustainable practices. AI models can predict fashion trends, reducing the uncertainty and resultant waste from unsold stock. Moreover, AI aids in creating digital samples, which cuts down the need for physical prototypes, significantly lowering fabric waste.

AI's application in waste management is another transformative aspect. Retail stores generate significant waste from unsold goods and packaging. AI-driven waste sorting systems improve recycling processes by using advanced image recognition to sort items with greater precision and speed. This ensures that more materials are correctly recycled, thus reducing the amount of waste that ends up in landfills.

Moreover, AI helps in tailoring sustainability messages to consumers. Retailers are utilizing AI to analyze consumer preferences and tailor sustainability-related communications that better align with customer values, enhancing engagement and loyalty. Personalized marketing strategies informed by AI insights can promote eco-friendly products more effectively and foster a culture of sustainability among consumers.

In addition, AI empowers retailers to create more sustainable supply chains by enhancing transparency. Through blockchain integration, AI can offer end-to-end visibility, allowing customers to trace the journey of a product from its origin to its shelf. This transparency not only helps in verifying ethical sourcing but also reinforces consumer trust and a brand's commitment to sustainability.

While the benefits of AI in promoting sustainable practices are significant, it's crucial to acknowledge the responsibility that comes with it. Implementing AI solutions requires careful consideration of ethical implications and the potential for unintended environmental impacts, such as energy consumption by data centers powering AI technologies. Therefore, integrating AI with renewable energy sources and maximizing its efficiency remains a priority for sustainable development in retail.

In conclusion, AI's role in sustainable retail practices is multifaceted and impactful, providing tools and technologies that enable retailers to operate more efficiently, reduce their carbon footprint, and meet the increasing demand for sustainable products and practices. As the retail industry continues to embrace this change, the synergy between AI and sustainability not only promises to reshape commerce but also sets the stage for a more responsible and environmentally friendly future.

Chapter 18:
Cross-Channel Retail Strategies

As we explore the evolving landscape of retail, cross-channel strategies stand at the forefront of innovation, threading the needle between traditional and digital realms to redefine consumer interactions. By leveraging the power of AI, retailers are crafting seamless omnichannel experiences that blur the lines between online and offline, ensuring a cohesive journey across all touchpoints. This integration isn't just about meeting consumers where they are; it's about anticipating their needs and preferences in real-time, thus enhancing satisfaction and loyalty. The harmony between physical stores and digital platforms creates a dynamic ecosystem where data flows effortlessly, allowing for the customization and agility necessary in today's competitive market. As AI continues to mature, its role in bridging these channels becomes pivotal, not only optimizing the business model but also reshaping the future blueprint of retail engagement.

Omnichannel Experience with AI

At the core of a seamless retail experience lies the ability to bridge the physical and digital worlds—a concept termed as the "omnichannel experience." This paradigm shift, driven by advances in AI, is not only reshaping consumer expectations but also redefining how businesses interact with their customers. In this context, AI plays a pivotal role in harmonizing these interfaces, ensuring that all channels, whether online or offline, operate in unison.

Imagine walking into a store and the staff already knows your preferences due to your online browsing history. It's not a mere coincidence; it's the magic of AI. Companies are leveraging sophisticated algorithms to create this unified experience, personalizing interactions at every touchpoint. By analyzing data from diverse channels, AI can learn from consumer behaviors, predict spending patterns, and offer tailored recommendations that enhance the shopping journey.

Omnichannel strategies infused with AI are particularly compelling because they allow customers to transition from one channel to another without losing context. Whether a consumer starts researching a product on their smartphone, continues the journey on a desktop, and then completes the purchase in a physical store, their path remains fluid and cohesive. AI ensures that retailers maintain a single, consistent customer profile across all platforms and interactions.

The power of AI in enhancing the omnichannel experience also extends to inventory management and supply chain optimization, which are discussed in earlier chapters. In an omnichannel world, it's crucial for stock levels to be consistent across the board. AI solutions provide real-time data that helps retailers ensure this consistency, minimizing the risk of overselling and improving customer satisfaction.

As retailers adopt these AI-driven omnichannel strategies, they face the challenge of integrating disparate systems. It requires a tech-savvy mindset and often involves the restructuring of existing platforms. Retailers must ensure that their technological infrastructure is robust enough to handle vast amounts of data and complex algorithmic processes. This technological foundation is pivotal in synchronizing online and offline customer interactions.

Moreover, AI is vital in capturing consumer data and synthesizing insights, helping retailers understand how different channels influence purchasing decisions. For instance, AI can analyze patterns to ascertain why a consumer might research products online but opt to purchase in-store. These insights enable companies to tweak their strategies, making them more attuned to customer needs and increasing conversion rates.

In practice, the benefits of AI in creating a seamless omnichannel experience are vast. Consider the implementation of AI-powered chatbots, which provide 24/7 customer service across channels. Such tools not only enhance user engagement but also free up human resources for more complex tasks, ultimately boosting efficiency and improving the overall consumer experience.

Furthermore, cutting-edge technologies like augmented reality (AR) and virtual reality (VR) augment the omnichannel experience by offering immersive ways to interact with products without physical limitations. These AI applications provide a preview of the future, where the lines between digital and physical continue to blur, making shopping more intuitive and personalized than ever before.

This evolution towards AI-driven omnichannel solutions isn't just about keeping up with trends. It's about anticipating consumer needs and staying ahead in a highly competitive market. Businesses that embrace this approach position themselves as leaders, capable of delivering experiences that delight and retain customers.

The journey to an effective omnichannel strategy, however, is not without its hurdles. Integrating AI into existing systems requires investment and careful planning. It involves balancing technology upgrades with practical considerations such as staff training and consumer privacy concerns. The latter is particularly significant, as consumers demand transparency and control over their personal data.

In conclusion, AI is transforming the retail landscape by facilitating integrated, personalized, and efficient shopping experiences across all channels. The successful execution of an AI-driven omnichannel strategy relies on a company's ability to harness data, leverage technology, and understand consumer behavior. With the stakes higher than ever, retailers must strive to offer experiences that not only meet but exceed the evolving expectations of their customers, thereby securing their place in the future of retail.

Bridging Online and Offline Retail

In a rapidly evolving retail landscape, the convergence of online and offline channels is no longer just an innovation—it's a necessity. As retailers search for ways to remain relevant and competitive, the concept of seamless integration across these channels has emerged as a strategic imperative. This amalgamation promises not only to enhance customer experience but also to drive sales and growth, combining the best elements of digital engagement with the tangible, tactile world of physical retail.

At the heart of this cross-channel strategy are tools powered by artificial intelligence (AI). They unlock insights into consumer preferences and behaviors that traditional methods could never fully capture. By leveraging AI, retailers can create personalized experiences that resonate on an individual level with customers whether they're shopping from the comfort of their homes or visiting a store. The magic lies in AI's ability to interpret vast amounts of data, allowing for a smooth transition between channels and ensuring that every customer interaction feels cohesive and meaningful.

One potent example of bridging online and offline retail is found in data synchronization. Retailers now use AI to maintain a single, unified data source, ensuring consistency across each customer's digital and physical experiences. When a shopper adds an item to their online wishlist, visits a store, and receives a personalized offer, they're experiencing a well-orchestrated blend, propelled by the seamless integration of data and AI-driven insights.

In-store, AI solutions provide personalized recommendations to shoppers. Through advanced analytics, these systems understand not just what a customer might need, but when they might need it, effectively combining the immediacy of the online experience with the sensory opportunities of the physical world. This personalized assistance is as if the brand is saying, "We know you, and we're here to help—right here, right now."

The integration of AI doesn't stop with customer-facing tools. Behind the scenes, inventory management benefits tremendously from this approach. AI helps ensure that the products available online match those physically present in stores, minimizing disappointed customers who might find their desired items out of stock in a single channel. Through anticipated demand forecasting and real-time stock monitoring, retailers can maintain optimal stock levels, thus supporting a truly integrated shopping experience.

Additionally, AI-driven chatbots are closing the gap between online and offline retail by transcending physical limitations. These virtual assistants provide real-time support, bridging the channels by answering in-store queries about online products or processing online orders from within the physical store. This kind of integration not only boosts customer satisfaction but also encourages engagement with the brand across all channels.

Moreover, AI is playing a crucial role in enhancing in-store experiences with interactive displays and IoT devices. These technologies transform store visits into immersive experiences that echo the convenience and adaptability of online shopping. Imagine smart mirrors that suggest outfits based on previous online searches, or kiosks that allow customers to seamlessly transition from browsing in-store to purchasing online, should an item be unavailable on-site.

Another compelling idea is the use of AI in deploying efficient, personalized marketing strategies. By analyzing both online behavior and in-store engagements, retailers can craft targeted promotions that speak directly to a customer's interests, no matter where they choose to shop. This level of customization helps bridge any gap a customer might perceive between their online and offline experiences, making each touchpoint feel like part of the same unique journey tailored just for them.

The future of retail lies in the ability to offer an omnichannel experience in a world that's continuously shifting towards digital. AI allows retailers to enhance this journey by ensuring that a customer moving between channels feels continuity. This will not only foster loyalty but also open new avenues for growth and innovation as companies continue to explore what it means to create truly hybrid shopping experiences.

The convergence of online and offline retail, powered by AI, is more than just a technological trend. It's a fundamental shift in how we think about shopping itself, demanding a reevaluation of customer connections and the experience of discovering and purchasing products. Retailers who seize this opportunity to integrate and bridge these worlds will find themselves not only meeting customer needs but also shaping the future of shopping in profoundly new ways.

As the retail industry continues to navigate this transformation, the support of tools that blend digital efficiency with personal, physical interaction remains vital. Whether in establishing a more dynamic catalog, offering personalized services, or optimizing operational efficiency, AI stands as the keystone of this new era. By bridging online and offline channels, retail pioneers have a chance to redefine commerce, making it more integrated, intuitive, and indispensable than ever before.

Chapter 19:
AI in Marketing and Advertising

The integration of AI in marketing and advertising has become a game-changer for professionals striving to stand out in today's competitive landscape. By leveraging sophisticated algorithms and machine learning, businesses can now craft highly targeted marketing campaigns that resonate deeply with individual consumer preferences and behaviors. AI's capacity to analyze vast quantities of data enables advertisers to optimize ad spend efficiently, ensuring every dollar contributes to maximum ROI. This ability to tailor messaging and adjust strategies in real time empowers marketers to engage audiences with unprecedented precision and relevance. The synergy between AI and marketing doesn't just enhance customer relationships—it revolutionizes them, ushering in an era where conversational commerce and dynamic consumer engagement are the norms, not the exceptions. Through such advancements, AI is transforming marketing from an art of persuasion into a precise science of understanding, predicting, and meeting consumer needs in innovative ways.

Targeted Marketing Campaigns

Imagine walking into a store and seeing products displayed that seem almost as if they were picked exclusively for you. This is no accident. In the age of artificial intelligence, targeted marketing campaigns are not just about luck or general patterns but rather precision and personalization. AI's impact excites marketers with its potential to transform consumer interactions, shifting from broadcasting generic messages to engaging in conversations that feel intimate and attentive.

At the heart of these campaigns is data—massive amounts of it. AI systems are fed a near-infinite stream of information gathered from consumers' online and offline behaviors. This data covers purchase history, browsing habits, social media interactions, and more. Through advanced algorithms, AI can analyze this data in real-time, detecting subtle patterns and trends that would be nearly impossible for human analysts to identify on their own.

Notably, AI doesn't just provide insights; it acts on them. Marketers can use AI to design dynamic advertisements that adjust content according to the viewer's interests and demographics. The same goes for email marketing campaigns—AI helps in crafting messages that resonate on a personal level, increasing the likelihood of engagement. Gone are the days when ads simply relied on broad age or gender categories. Now, AI enables campaigns that are tailored to specific consumer personas, enhancing relevance and effectiveness.

What makes AI-powered targeted marketing truly revolutionary is its ability to predict consumer behavior. By employing machine learning models, AI can forecast a shopper's next move with surprising accuracy. Consider the case of a consumer who frequently browses tech gadgets. AI can anticipate when that person is likely contemplating a purchase, triggering a personalized offer or recommendation that can nudge them toward completing the transaction. Such predictive capabilities mean businesses not only meet customer needs but often precede them.

The power of AI in targeted marketing extends beyond mere product recommendations. It influences pricing strategies through the integration of dynamic pricing models. These models analyze consumer demand, competitor pricing, and market conditions in real-time, allowing businesses to adjust prices in a way that maximizes profitability while still satisfying consumer expectations. This synergy between marketing and pricing strategies ensures that both are not only aligned but also reinforcing.

Additionally, AI aids in segmenting audiences in ways that maximize campaign success. Traditional segmentation often relies on basic demographics, but AI-based segmentation delves deeper, creating micro-segments based on behavioral patterns, psychographics, and transaction history. This amplifies marketing effectiveness as messages can be crafted and delivered uniquely to each segment, essentially speaking the consumer's language. Brands that adopt these sophisticated methods are witnessing remarkable increases in conversion rates and customer loyalty.

The integration of AI in marketing campaigns facilitates deeper consumer understanding, helping businesses engage customers on a more personal level. However, with great power comes great responsibility. Businesses must be transparent about how they use customer data, ensuring ethical practices and adherence to privacy laws. Earning consumer trust is paramount, especially when leveraging data that feels intensely personal.

As more businesses embrace AI-driven marketing campaigns, challenges and opportunities will surface in equal measure. Marketers must continuously refine AI models to mitigate biases that could inadvertently skew campaigns and lead to misleading conclusions. Balancing automation with the human touch will remain an essential part of ensuring campaigns do not feel too mechanical or intrusive.

Despite the challenges, AI's potential to revolutionize marketing and advertising remains immense. By crafting campaigns that are not only smart but also adaptive and sensitive to individual consumers, businesses can genuinely transform their customer connections. As AI continues to evolve, the future promises even more innovative approaches to marketing that could redefine how consumers experience and engage with brands.

Thus, in the realm of targeted marketing, AI is not just an accessory but a fundamental cornerstone. It offers a glimpse into a future where marketing is as much about understanding as it is about selling. As brands harness the power of AI to engage consumers in meaningful ways, the relationship between businesses and consumers will likely deepen, becoming more reciprocal and mutually beneficial than ever before.

Optimizing Ad Spend with AI

In the rapidly evolving landscape of retail, effective advertising stands as a pillar of success. As competition intensifies and consumer attention becomes increasingly fragmented, businesses must pivot their strategies to maximize the impact of their advertising efforts. This is where artificial intelligence (AI) steps in, offering transformative capabilities for optimizing ad spend, enabling retailers to connect with their audience more efficiently and economically.

AI's venture into advertising isn't just about number crunching; it's about predicting human behaviors, understanding customer nuances, and adapting to fluid market dynamics. By harnessing AI, retailers can extract actionable insights from vast oceanic data pools, aligning their ad strategies with consumer preferences. This data-driven approach empowers businesses to transform intuition-based decisions into precision-targeted campaigns.

The essence of AI in ad spend optimization lies in its ability to process complex datasets with remarkable speed and accuracy. AI algorithms sift through customer behavior data, demographic details, purchasing history, and even social media interactions. The insights drawn from these analyses guide businesses in creating hyper-personalized ad content, ensuring that messages resonate with the target audience. As a result, ad campaigns morph into conversations that are both relevant and engaging.

One of AI's standout features in this realm is predictive analytics. By leveraging machine learning algorithms, businesses can forecast future advertising performance and allocate budgets to high-impact areas. This predictive prowess minimizes wasted ad spend and enhances return on investment (ROI). Imagine a world where every dollar spent on advertising is strategically placed to yield maximum output—that's the promise of AI.

Furthermore, AI optimizes ad creative through iterative testing and refinement. Through AI-driven A/B testing, various versions of advertisements can be evaluated, with the AI seamlessly determining which variants perform best. This continuous feedback loop enables marketers to refine their creatives without the guesswork, crafting ads that strike the right chord with consumers.

Programmatic advertising, powered by AI, also plays a pivotal role in ad spend optimization. Programmatic platforms use AI algorithms to automate the buying and placement of ads in real time, targeting the most appropriate customers across diverse channels. This automation not only streamlines processes but also ensures the precise targeting of audiences with contextually relevant ads, maximizing campaign effectiveness.

Furthermore, AI aids in optimizing ad timing—a critical aspect often overlooked. By understanding when a target audience is most receptive, AI systems can schedule ads for times that promise greater engagement. This ensures that the message reaches the right audience at the right moment, significantly boosting engagement rates and conversion likelihood.

In the realm of cost-efficiency, AI-driven solutions exhibit their prowess by identifying and eliminating ad fraud. Click fraud, a phenomenon where invalid clicks inflate ad metrics, has long plagued advertisers. AI employs advanced algorithms to detect anomalies and safeguard investments, allowing businesses to channel resources to genuine interactions. This vigilance ensures that the advertising budget is allocated wisely, reducing wastage and enhancing ad performance.

Yet, optimizing ad spend with AI is not without its challenges. The sheer volume of data necessitates robust infrastructure and advanced computing capabilities. Additionally, integrating AI systems with existing advertising tools can be technically demanding. Businesses must navigate these challenges to unlock AI's full potential in ad budget optimization.

However, the benefits far outweigh the hurdles. AI in advertising not only leads to better resource allocation but also provides marketers with a nuanced understanding of consumer behaviors. This intelligence allows businesses to craft marketing strategies that are agile, responsive, and future-ready.

The ethical considerations of AI in marketing shouldn't be overlooked, though. Retailers must ensure that their data handling practices are transparent and respect consumer privacy. As AI continues integrating into ad spend frameworks, businesses should prioritize ethical standards, assuring consumers that their data is managed responsibly.

Ultimately, AI is reshaping how retailers think about ad spend. It offers a rich toolkit for achieving precision targeting, optimizing budgets, and delivering meaningful consumer interactions. As the retail landscape continues its digital transformation, those who embrace AI-driven ad strategies will undoubtedly forge a competitive edge, standing out in a crowded market.

In every click, view, and conversion lies an opportunity to learn and improve. AI not only facilitates this learning but accelerates it, opening doors to new possibilities in advertising excellence. As we look to the future, the intersection of AI and ad spend optimization will continue to evolve, driving impactful innovations and guiding the retail industry's march towards a more intelligent, consumer-centric world.

Chapter 20:
Challenges and Risks of AI Adoption

As the retail industry embraces the transformative potential of AI, it inevitably faces a variety of challenges and risks that must be navigated thoughtfully. Technical integration issues often present the first hurdle, as legacy systems may not easily mesh with sophisticated AI technologies, requiring substantial investment and innovation to overcome. Additionally, enterprises must address consumer trust issues, especially regarding data security and privacy, to foster a loyal customer base amidst growing concerns about data misuse. Balancing these risks, businesses need to instill transparency and foster a culture of ethical AI use to mitigate fear and resistance, potentially turning these challenges into opportunities for growth. Success in this arena demands a strategic approach that integrates cutting-edge technologies while maintaining the human touch that has always been at the heart of retail, ensuring that AI serves as a catalyst for enhancement rather than a point of contention.

Overcoming Technical Barriers

AI adoption in retail promises a transformative journey, but it is fraught with technical hurdles that must be skillfully navigated. One of the most pressing concerns is infrastructure readiness. Many traditional retail systems are not built to handle the data-intensive processes that AI requires. Therefore, investing in robust hardware and scalable cloud solutions is non-negotiable for seamless AI integration.

Retailers need to upgrade legacy systems to provide the necessary computing power and speed, ensuring that data flows smoothly across platforms for timely decision-making.

Another significant challenge is data quality. AI thrives on vast, diverse, and clean datasets, yet many retail data landscapes are fragmented and inconsistent. Solutions start with a comprehensive data management strategy, which includes effective data cleaning, integration, and governance. Retailers must prioritize the aggregation of data from multiple sources, creating unified data ecosystems that AI models can tap into. This coherence allows for better analysis and more reliable AI-driven insights.

Scalability, too, is a critical factor. Retail businesses vary greatly in size, each requiring different levels of AI scaling. Small and midsize retailers may not need the extensive AI frameworks larger operations do, but scalability should still factor into their approaches. Flexible, cloud-based solutions allow businesses to scale AI capabilities up or down, aligning with company growth or fluctuating demand. This flexibility is essential in adjusting to seasonal shopping patterns or unexpected retail trends.

Integration can often present another barrier. Many retailers already use different software solutions for inventory, sales, marketing, and customer relations. Integrating AI into these systems without disrupting existing operations can pose a significant challenge. Custom APIs and middleware can serve as solutions, ensuring that AI systems communicate effectively with existing infrastructure. Such integrations must be designed to minimize downtime and maintain data consistency across various platforms.

Next, we arrive at the challenge of algorithmic transparency and bias. AI technologies can inadvertently perpetuate or even exacerbate biases present in training data. Retailers need to implement measures for reviewing and auditing algorithms regularly, identifying potential biases, and rectifying them promptly. Collaboration with AI ethics committees and third-party audits can ensure that AI systems remain fair, transparent, and accountable to both businesses and consumers.

Understanding AI technologies and their appropriate applications is crucial. Many retail executives lack comprehensive knowledge of AI, hindering informed decision-making. Developing internal expertise is key, either through hiring tech talent experienced in AI or upskilling current employees. AI literacy programs can help demystify the technology, enabling staff and leaders to make strategic decisions that align with technological capabilities and retail goals.

Security and privacy present further roadblocks in AI adoption. Retailers must safeguard sensitive customer information, especially given the rise of data breaches. Implementing strong cybersecurity measures and compliance frameworks is essential to protect against threats and ensure regulatory adherence. Encryption and access controls should be part of a comprehensive strategy to secure both consumer data and proprietary company information.

Despite these challenges, overcoming technical barriers to AI adoption isn't an insurmountable task. It requires a nuanced approach, one that balances technological advancements with human oversight and strategic foresight. By addressing each barrier with targeted solutions and creating pathways for ongoing adaptation and learning, retailers can harness AI's full potential.

Embracing AI isn't just about integrating new technologies; it's also about fostering a culture open to innovation. Leaders must cultivate a forward-thinking mindset within their organizations, ensuring every team member sees AI as a tool for enhancement rather than a threat. This can be achieved through initiatives that celebrate AI-driven successes and reshape corporate narratives around technology's role in retail.

The reality of AI's transformative power in retail becomes evident as technical barriers are systematically dismantled. By establishing a robust technical foundation, retailers pave the way for more personalized shopping experiences, optimized operations, and sustained competitive advantages. As the journey unfolds, retailers will find that the rewards of overcoming technical barriers far outweigh the initial hurdles, driving a new era of AI-empowered commerce.

Addressing Consumer Trust Issues

As artificial intelligence continues to reshape the retail landscape, one of the most pressing challenges is the issue of consumer trust. Retailers are increasingly relying on AI to enhance customer experiences, streamline operations, and improve decision-making. However, amidst these advancements, consumers are becoming more concerned about how their personal data is being used and the extent to which AI influences their shopping journeys.

Consumer trust is foundational to the success of any retailer. A breach in this trust can result in significant repercussions, not just in terms of lost sales but also in damaged reputations and brand loyalty. For AI to be a beneficial tool rather than a contentious one, retailers must actively address the skepticism that surrounds its use, particularly concerning data security and privacy.

Transparency plays a critical role in bridging the trust gap. Consumers want to understand what data is being collected, why it's needed, and how it will be used. Providing clear and accessible information regarding data handling policies can demystify AI processes. By doing so, retailers can empower consumers, enabling them to make informed choices about their data-sharing preferences.

Moreover, incorporating user-friendly consent mechanisms can further bolster consumer confidence. Simplified opt-in and opt-out options allow consumers to maintain control over their personal information, fostering a sense of empowerment rather than intrusion. When people feel they have agency over their data, their willingness to engage with AI-driven systems naturally increases.

Transparency alone isn't enough. Retailers must also demonstrate accountability. Establishing consistent procedures for addressing data breaches and privacy violations is essential. Quick, transparent communication in the aftermath of a breach can help mitigate negative impacts and reassure customers that their concerns are taken seriously. Additionally, adopting robust encryption technologies and security measures can prevent potential data breaches from occurring in the first place.

Another dimension to consider is ensuring AI systems are free from biases that could alienate consumers. Bias in AI recommendations can skew purchasing scenarios, inadvertently discriminating against certain consumer groups. Retailers must continually audit their AI algorithms, removing biases and ensuring the systems reflect fairness and equity. By championing unbiased AI, companies reinforce their commitment to inclusivity and fairness.

Beyond addressing data concerns and systemic bias, fostering a dialogue with consumers about AI and its role in the retail experience can further enhance trust. Open forums, Q&A sessions, and educational content about AI can demystify the technology, making it more approachable for the average consumer. When consumers understand the tangible benefits AI can bring to their shopping experiences—be it through personalized recommendations or streamlined checkout processes—they're likely to engage with it more positively.

Retailers should also explore collaboration with third-party entities to certify their AI systems' ethical compliance and transparency. Certifications from independent organizations can serve as trust badges, signaling to consumers that a retailer's AI use meets high ethical standards. This external validation can be powerful in enhancing consumer confidence.

While technology evolves, human elements of customer service remain vital. AI should not replace these human interactions but rather complement them. Ensure customers have ample access to human representatives who can address their concerns and queries, particularly for complex issues that AI systems may not be equipped to handle. Maintaining a hybrid approach can reassure consumers that while AI enhances efficiency, the brand values human touch.

Investment in employee training regarding AI ethics and data privacy can further solidify consumer trust. Employees well-versed in these areas serve as ambassadors for the brand's values, able to articulate the benefits and safeguards associated with AI. Well-trained staff can play a significant role in addressing consumer apprehensions, cultivating a culture of trust from within the organization.

Ultimately, building trust in AI requires a multi-faceted approach. Retailers must be proactive, not reactive, in fortifying consumer trust. They must engage consumers in meaningful dialogue, offering reassurance and clarity about AI technologies. By balancing innovation with responsibility, retailers can harness the full potential of AI to enhance retail experiences while upholding consumer trust.

Chapter 21:
Future Innovations in AI for Retail

The retail landscape is on the brink of revolutionary shifts, driven by emerging technologies that promise to redefine the shopping experience as we know it. With anticipation building around cutting-edge advancements in AI, such as quantum computing and advanced machine learning algorithms, retailers are gearing up for a wave of possibilities that could transform everything from how consumers interact with brands to the architecture of supply chains. Imagine intelligent stores equipped with AI-powered robots that not only manage inventory but also provide personalized customer service, or virtual fitting rooms enhanced by augmented reality, allowing shoppers to experience apparel in a lifelike manner without physical trials. The integration of AI with blockchain technology holds potential for unprecedented levels of transparency and efficiency in product sourcing and delivery. As these innovations emerge, retailers who embrace and adapt to these technologies will likely set the standard for future consumer expectations and operational excellence, ushering in a new era of intelligent commerce. The convergence of AI with other disruptive technologies serves not only as a catalyst for innovation but also as an inspiring call to action for retail leaders to pioneer these frontiers, ensuring they remain at the forefront of this transformative journey.

Emerging Technologies

In the rapidly evolving landscape of AI, emerging technologies in retail hold the promise to redefine how consumers interact with brands and products. While current AI applications have already reshaped many facets of the retail world, the technologies bubbling up promise to catalyze even more profound changes. From quantum computing enhancing AI capabilities to neural networks mimicking human cognitive processes more closely, these tech innovations stand at the brink of mainstream application, offering retailers and consumers entirely new paradigms of interaction.

Quantum computing, although still in its nascent stages, has the potential to revolutionize AI processing speeds and capabilities. The implications for retail are manifold. With quantum computers, AI systems could analyze vast datasets at unprecedented speeds. Imagine a retail environment where customer data is processed in real-time at such a depth and breadth that product recommendations become almost telepathic. Retailers will potentially achieve instantaneous micro-targeting, offering customized experiences that traditional systems could only dream of. This technology could refine inventory predictions or customer preferences to astonishing levels of accuracy.

Another promising technology is the advancement of neuromorphic computing. This involves the development of chips that mimic the human brain's architecture, enabling AI systems to process information more like humans do. In retail, this could mean AI systems capable of understanding human emotions and nuances—transforming customer service interactions profoundly. AI could intuit customer feelings from subtle cues and adapt interactions accordingly, offering empathy-based solutions. Such progression could create retail experiences where AI isn't just a tool but evolves into a conversational partner, blurring the lines between human and machine interaction in stores or online.

The integration of AI within autonomous systems is another frontier with implications for the retail sector. Self-navigating delivery robots and drones are not merely the stuff of sci-fi anymore. These technologies could significantly enhance logistics and last-mile delivery, providing swifter and more economical solutions. While autonomous delivery vehicles are a topic of intense development and debate, their widespread adoption can drastically reduce delivery times and operational costs. Retailers stand to benefit notably by offering same-hour delivery services that were once considered logistically impossible.

Artificial general intelligence (AGI), while still theoretical at this stage, also holds potential to dramatically alter the retail landscape. Unlike current AI systems designed for specific tasks, AGI would perform any intellectual task a human can. In retail, this could translate into centralized AI systems executing various operations— from dynamic pricing strategies to emotional analysis, all simultaneously and seamlessly. Such a system promises to bring a level of sophistication and integration that contemporary AI solutions can't match, rendering retail operations more coherent and efficient.

Moreover, blockchain's role as an emerging technology in retail, combined with AI, cannot be ignored. It offers new ways of ensuring transparency and security in supply chains. Blockchain ledgers, when integrated with AI, could automate and authenticate transactions in real time, ensuring data remains untampered and verifiable. The trust factor, vital in customer data handling and tracking product origins, is exponentially enhanced. Blockchain's cryptographic nature ensures that customer data is safeguarded against breaches, fostering a safer ecosystem for the digital economy.

AI-driven robotics in physical retail spaces is another area poised for innovation with immense potential. In the near future, robots could manage inventory, restock shelves, and even offer in-store assistance to customers. These robots, equipped with advanced AI systems, could adapt to the store's unique ecosystem, learning optimal paths for efficiency in real-time, and ensuring stock levels align perfectly with predicted demand patterns. Practical benefits include significantly reducing human resource needs for mundane tasks while elevating customer service levels.

Lastly, as 5G technology continues its global rollout, it promises to further amplify AI capabilities in retail. The ultra-fast data transfers and minimal latency offered by 5G networks will enable real-time, cloud-based AI decision making at the edge. Retailers can leverage this capability to deliver lightning-fast customer experiences, from AR and VR applications in showrooms to hyper-responsive mobile apps guiding in-store navigation. The efficiency of data handling in cashless and contactless payments will further boost customer convenience and satisfaction.

In conclusion, the trajectory of emerging AI technologies primes the retail industry for unprecedented transformation. As these technologies mature, they will push boundaries and redefine the relationship between retailers and their customers. Opportunities abound for businesses that remain nimble and proactive, ready to adapt and harness these innovations. While challenges of integration and ethics persist, the potential for creating seamless, personalized, and intelligent retail experiences is boundless. The future of retail lies not just in catching up with technology, but in embracing and advancing these emerging paradigms.

The Next Frontier in Shopping Experiences

As we delve into the next frontier of shopping experiences, it's clear that the confluence of emerging technologies is set to redefine the retail landscape. Today, AI stands at the helm of this transformation, poised to deliver an experience that feels not just futuristic but almost magical. Imagine walking into a store where every product adjusts its display personalized to your habits, preferences, and even mood. This vision is becoming possible thanks to the advances in AI, and it's revolutionizing how we interact with retail environments.

At the core of this transformation is AI's ability to provide hyper-personalization. While the concept of personalized shopping isn't new, the scale and precision with which AI can tailor experiences is unprecedented. Machine learning algorithms can now analyze vast amounts of data to predict consumer behavior, anticipate needs, and deliver personalized recommendations with astonishing accuracy. The ability to integrate past purchase history, real-time browsing patterns, and emerging trends allows AI systems to craft shopping experiences that are uniquely tailored for each customer.

We're entering an era where AI doesn't just react, it anticipates. Predictive analytics combined with advanced machine learning enables the retail sector to forecast not only what a consumer might want today but also what they'll desire tomorrow. This predictive power is key to creating seamless shopping journeys that feel both intuitive and satisfying. Retailers are using AI to curate not just products, but entire experiences that feel bespoke to the individual, crafting a narrative that speaks directly to them.

Further pushing the frontier are immersive technologies, such as virtual and augmented reality, which are intersecting with AI to create unparalleled retail experiences. These technologies are no longer gimmicks; they are tools that enhance how consumers interact with products and brands. AI-driven VR and AR applications enable customers to visualize products in their own environments, offering a preview that closes the gap between online convenience and in-store tangibility. This layer of interaction allows shoppers to engage more deeply, fostering a connection that was previously hard to achieve online.

Moreover, the role of AI in nurturing emotional engagement can't be overlooked. Retailers are leveraging AI to understand emotional cues through natural language processing and sentiment analysis. This allows businesses to respond to customer queries and preferences with empathy and precision, enhancing satisfaction and loyalty. By recognizing not just what customers are saying, but how they're feeling, AI can customize interactions to be more human-like, creating a bridge between technology and personal connection.

The physical store isn't being left behind; it's evolving alongside these digital trends. Smart stores powered by the Internet of Things (IoT) and AI are becoming the new norm. These stores use sensors and AI to optimize everything from inventory to customer service. For instance, AI algorithms help manage cashierless checkouts, track customer movements to optimize store layouts, and provide real-time stock levels that ensure products are always available. This blend of AI with in-store technology ensures that the retail experience is not only efficient but also enriching.

As we explore this frontier, AI is also dismantling traditional barriers and creating opportunities for inclusivity in retail. By utilizing voice recognition and language processing, AI-driven platforms are becoming more accessible, breaking down communication barriers for diverse language speakers and those with disabilities. Designing interfaces that everyone can use, irrespective of their physical or linguistic abilities, isn't just a technological advancement; it's a societal imperative. AI breathes life into strategies that make shopping a universally welcoming experience.

The confluence of AI and sustainable practices presents another exciting frontier. Retailers are under increasing pressure to adopt environmentally sound practices, and AI provides the tools to do so efficiently. Through advanced data modeling, AI can optimize supply chains, predict inventory needs to minimize waste, and even influence responsible consumer behavior through smart recommendations. This not only helps retailers align with green initiatives but also enhances brand loyalty among increasingly eco-conscious consumers.

However, the journey toward these innovations isn't without its challenges. The complexity of implementing sophisticated AI solutions requires strategic planning and investment. Retailers must balance the opportunities AI presents with the ethical considerations it demands. Privacy concerns, data security, and the potential for algorithmic bias all present hurdles that must be navigated carefully. Yet, addressing these issues head-on will only strengthen the role of AI in crafting the future of retail.

As we glance at the horizon, it's apparent that the next frontier in shopping experiences is not about merely adding technology to existing frameworks. It's about fundamentally rethinking the essence of retail and reshaping it in a way that is smart, sustainable, and phenomenally personal. The potential lies in seamlessly blending AI with human insights to create spaces where commerce isn't just a transaction but a transformative experience.

In conclusion, AI's transformative potential in retail extends into numerous facets of the shopping experience, each more exciting and boundary-pushing than the last. From hyper-personalization to immersive interactivity, the road ahead is not only about technological advancement but about enriching the human experience in commerce. As retailers embrace these innovations, they stand on the cusp of a new era, one where the blend of AI and creativity will define the next chapter in the retail narrative.

Chapter 22:
Global Perspectives on AI in Retail

As AI technologies weave deeper into the fabric of retail, their influence stretches well beyond any single locale, crafting a dynamic global landscape. In every corner of the world, AI adoption patterns reflect diverse economic priorities, consumer expectations, and cultural nuances. For instance, in Asia, where digital-first shopping habits are the norm, AI is enhancing hyper-personalized consumer experiences. In contrast, European markets focus on AI applications that balance innovation with stringent data privacy regulations. Meanwhile, North America is pioneering cutting-edge retail tech that blends AI with immersive experiences. Yet, despite these regional differences, a shared vision emerges: AI as a pivotal force reshaping commerce to boost efficiency and creativity while fostering new ways of engaging consumers across continents. Adapting AI tools for varied markets requires a nuanced approach, ensuring solutions are resilient enough to handle both emerging market challenges and established economic landscapes. The global exchange of ideas and technologies in AI-driven retail promises not just to redefine shopping but also to converge diverse markets towards a future characterized by intelligent, seamless, and culturally attuned commerce.

Regional Trends and Developments

As AI continues to revolutionize the retail sector globally, distinct regional trends and developments have begun to emerge, each influenced by unique market dynamics, consumer preferences, and technological infrastructure. Understanding these regional trends is crucial for retailers aiming to harness AI's full potential while ensuring relevance and competitiveness in diverse markets.

In North America, AI adoption in retail has been robust, driven by a highly competitive market landscape and an innovation-friendly regulatory environment. Retail giants like Amazon and Walmart are pioneering AI research, setting benchmarks in supply chain optimization and customer personalization. These companies leverage AI to enhance service delivery, tailor marketing strategies, and streamline operations. North American retailers are investing heavily in AI-driven technologies, prioritizing advancements such as machine learning algorithms for dynamic pricing and AI-powered chatbots for customer service. The region's consumers, accustomed to rapid technological change, display a high acceptance level of AI-powered retail experiences, favoring innovation that adds convenience and personalization to their shopping journey.

Conversely, Europe shows a varied pace of AI adoption across its countries, heavily influenced by stringent data privacy laws like the General Data Protection Regulation (GDPR). European retailers navigate complex regulatory landscapes while integrating AI, emphasizing ethical AI practices and consumer data protection. This regulatory focus has led to innovative solutions that balance personalization and privacy. Market leaders in countries like Germany and the UK are renowned for implementing sophisticated AI systems tailored to cater to local market conditions. European consumers, generally more cautious about data privacy, have prompted retailers to explore AI applications that ensure transparency and trust, fostering an environment where ethical AI usage propels retail innovation).

In Asia, the scene is markedly different, with countries like China and India at the forefront of AI implementation in retail. These countries benefit from a vast pool of technical talent and a thriving startup ecosystem that champions rapid technological adoption. China, in particular, boasts some of the world's most advanced AI-driven retail technologies, with companies like Alibaba and JD.com leading the charge. Their smart stores, equipped with facial recognition and AI-driven logistics, redefine consumer shopping experiences, offering unprecedented levels of personalization and convenience. Meanwhile, in India, AI facilitates bridging the urban-rural retail divide. Retailers employ AI to understand diverse consumer preferences, consequently expanding market reach and optimizing supply chains to address logistical challenges inherent to the region.

Across Africa, AI in retail presents tremendous potential for transforming traditional markets. Although still in the nascent stages of development, AI-powered solutions are gaining traction, especially in areas like mobile payment systems and customer engagement platforms. Nigerian and South African retailers are early adopters, leveraging AI to enhance inventory management and customer interaction within limitations posed by infrastructural deficits. The young, tech-savvy population in many African nations underscores a future with significant AI adoption in retail, with regional trends steered by grassroots innovation and an ever-increasing internet penetration rate.

In Latin America, AI trends in retail revolve around addressing longstanding challenges such as market informality and payment system inefficiencies. Brazil and Mexico are at the forefront, integrating AI into e-commerce platforms to streamline operations and enrich customer experiences. The region is witnessing a digital transformation wave catalyzed by rising internet usage and smartphone proliferation, with AI spearheading retail innovations that enhance market inclusivity and customer personalization. Latin American retailers are increasingly partnering with international tech firms to imbibe best practices and leverage advanced AI tools that drive competitive edge in the global retail arena.

Meanwhile, in Oceania, particularly Australia and New Zealand, AI adoption is characterized by a focus on consumer-centric applications. Retailers emphasize enhancing the shopping experience by integrating AI into their loyalty programs, personalizing promotions, and refining supply chain processes to ensure faster delivery times. The region's approach reflects a commitment to sustainability, with AI applications designed to optimize resource use and minimize environmental impact—a critical consideration for conscious consumers in Oceania.

Despite these regional variances, several universal trends in AI adoption in retail cut across borders. The demand for AI-driven personalization—crafting unique shopping experiences for each customer—remains a significant focus globally. Retailers universally aim to optimize supply chains for efficiency, reduce operational costs with AI automation, and enrich customer service through AI-powered chat interfaces. Additionally, concerns over privacy and ethical AI deployment resonate worldwide as retailers navigate the delicate balance of innovation and consumer consent.

In summary, while regional developments in AI for retail reflect distinct market realities, they share a common theme: leveraging technology to enhance consumer experiences and operational efficiency. By understanding and adapting to these regional trends, retailers can align their AI strategies with local needs and preferences, ultimately driving global success in an increasingly competitive landscape. As AI continues to evolve, these regional dynamics will undoubtedly shape the future trajectory of retail innovation, fostering a retail ecosystem that is not only technologically advanced but also attuned to the diverse tapestry of global consumer expectations.

Adapting AI for Diverse Markets

In a rapidly evolving retail landscape molded by AI, the ability to adapt technologies for different markets is becoming a key competitive advantage. As businesses expand globally, they face a multitude of challenges, including differing consumer preferences, regulatory environments, and levels of technological infrastructure. AI, with its powerful customization capabilities, can be a bridge to understanding and thriving in these varied contexts. This section will explore how retailers can adeptly modify AI to meet the unique needs of international markets.

First, it's essential to understand that consumer expectations and behaviors are deeply rooted in cultural, social, and economic factors. AI systems designed for retail must reflect these diverse consumer landscapes. For example, a personalized shopping experience driven by AI in Japan may focus on minimalistic aesthetics and high-quality product recommendations, while in India, it might prioritize discounts and product bundling due to different consumer buying motivations. Such tailored experiences require an AI's underlying algorithms to be adapted by drawing insights from localized data patterns.

Localization goes beyond just language translation—it encompasses adapting to the nuances of cultural attitudes towards technology and shopping. For instance, in Western markets, consumers may be more accepting of AI-driven customer service interactions. In contrast, some Asian markets may prefer a blend of human and AI consultancy to maintain a personal touch. Thus, AI systems must be flexible: they need to comprehensively understand both structured data and subtle, unstructured data such as local dialect sentiment and non-verbal cues.

Regulatory frameworks present another significant consideration when adapting AI for diverse markets. Countries like the European Union have stringent data protection laws, such as the General Data

Protection Regulation (GDPR), which dictate how consumer data can be collected and used. In contrast, other regions might have more relaxed regulations or different priorities, such as fostering innovation and digital adoption. Retailers must ensure their AI systems comply with these differing regulations, safeguarding against potential legal implications while maintaining consumer trust worldwide.

Also crucial is the adaptation to technological variability. Retailers need to consider the technological infrastructure in different regions, which can range from high-speed, ubiquitous internet connectivity in urban areas to limited access in rural locations. AI solutions that are heavily reliant on cloud-based processing may need alternatives like edge computing, which processes data near the source, to be viable in areas with less reliable internet connections. This technological flexibility ensures that AI solutions remain operational and effective across varied market conditions.

AI's role extends to supply chain and logistics, which are critical components of retail that often require adaptation to the local market conditions. In regions where the supply chain infrastructure is less mature, AI can optimize logistics by selecting the most efficient travel routes, predicting potential delays, and suggesting alternative suppliers. This adaptability ensures that businesses can remain competitive, delivering goods efficiently even in challenging environments.

Moreover, adapting AI for diverse markets involves strategic partnerships with local experts and vendors. Collaborating with local businesses helps AI systems incorporate authentic insights, ensuring recommendations and automated decisions are culturally sensitive and relevant. Partnerships can also facilitate quicker compliance with local laws and streamline supply chain integrations.

The capability of AI to analyze vast amounts of data quickly is its greatest strength in market adaptation. This capacity means that market research, which may take traditional methods months to gather and analyze, can be completed in days. This rapid insight generation enables retailers to respond promptly to market changes, adapting their strategies to meet shifting demands, such as those caused by economic fluctuations or emerging consumer trends.

Differentiation in marketing strategies across global markets is yet another domain where AI personalization pays dividends. AI-driven analytics enable businesses to understand which marketing messages resonate in different cultures and tailor campaigns accordingly. By leveraging data about local preferences and behavior patterns, retailers can craft and deliver messages that engage effectively and drive better ROI on marketing spend.

Finally, as AI technology matures, retailers must continuously train and develop their AI systems to recognize and adapt to new trends. Continuous learning loops will be essential to ensure AI systems are responsive to changes in consumer behavior, technological advancement, and policy shifts. This ability not only engenders competitive advantage but also builds the resilience needed to withstand the inevitable disruptions of an increasingly globalized retail environment.

In conclusion, as AI becomes further embedded in retail operations, its success in a global context hinges on adaptability. Each market presents unique challenges and opportunities, and only those organizations that effectively tailor their AI strategies to meet these diverse needs will thrive. By intelligently harnessing the power of AI, retailers can glean deeper insights, personalize customer interactions, and ultimately succeed in the multifaceted dynamics of international commerce.

Chapter 23:
Regulatory and Policy Implications

Navigating the regulatory and policy landscape is paramount for retailers leveraging AI, as it shapes the future of technology implementation and compliance strategies. With AI continually advancing, regulatory bodies worldwide are struggling to keep pace, necessitating forward-thinking approaches to potential legal challenges. Retailers must anticipate changes in data privacy laws, intellectual property rights, and ethical AI use, ensuring they align with evolving standards. A robust governance framework is critical; it requires a dynamic interplay of transparency, accountability, and compliance with international guidelines. As the lines between technology and commerce blur, businesses need to engage in proactive dialogues with policymakers to influence regulations that are both innovative-friendly and consumer-protective. By championing ethical considerations and immersive regulations, the industry can drive AI's transformative potential while fostering trust and security in this rapidly changing environment.

Navigating Legal Challenges

As the retail industry continuously integrates AI technologies to redefine consumer experiences and operational efficiencies, it inevitably encounters a labyrinth of legal obstacles. Navigating these legal challenges requires a nuanced understanding of a rapidly evolving landscape where technological innovation often outpaces legislation.

The stakes are high because these legal intricacies determine not just compliance but can influence innovation trajectories and competitive positioning in the market.

The first arena of legal challenge in AI for retail is data privacy and protection. As AI systems thirst for data to boost their algorithms, they run into the thick brush of privacy laws and regulations such as GDPR in Europe and CCPA in California. These regulations mandate stringent requirements for how consumer data is collected, processed, and stored. For retail businesses, ensuring compliance isn't just about avoiding fines. It's about earning and maintaining consumer trust. Companies must implement transparent data practices, requiring explicit consent and providing consumers with clear pathways to manage their personal information.

Consider the broader implications of failing to navigate these privacy concerns adeptly. A single data breach or violation can lead to severe penalties and a tarnished reputation that takes years, if not decades, to rebuild. Retailers must keep their finger on the pulse of regulatory updates and invest in cybersecurity measures that not only shield consumer data but also prevent unauthorized AI model training that could leverage sensitive information indiscriminately.

Another layer of legal complexity emerges around intellectual property (IP) rights. AI systems in retail, especially those involved in innovative design or creative marketing strategies, tread the fine line of IP law. Traditional IP frameworks struggle to define ownership and rights when creativity is AI-driven. Does an AI system deserve credit, or does the company owning the system claim rights to the creations? This legal gray area requires foresight and proactive policy-making to protect and capitalize on AI-driven innovations without running afoul of existing IP laws.

In the retail sector, where branding and distinctiveness can be game-changers, maintaining the integrity of trademarks and copyrighted materials while utilizing AI for content creation is paramount. Retailers must vigilantly safeguard their own IP while navigating AI tools that might inadvertently infringe on others' rights.

Employment law also enters the legal landscape as AI continues to reshape the workforce. The deployment of AI-driven systems in retail disrupts traditional labor patterns, leading to concerns about job displacement and the creation of unskilled and skilled human roles. Legal frameworks are struggling to keep up with the rapid pace at which AI is redefining roles, compensation, and employment standards. For retailers, constructing transparent policies that address workforce transformation is not just a legal obligation but a strategic necessity to ensure motivated and legally protected employees.

Moreover, there are anti-discrimination laws to consider. AI algorithms, if not carefully monitored and calibrated, can perpetuate or even exacerbate biases inherent in training data. Retailers utilizing AI for hiring, pricing, or customer service need robust mechanisms to prevent biases that could lead to discriminatory practices. This facet of AI legality is critically linked to corporate social responsibility and the broader commitment to equality and fairness in business practices.

Cross-border sales and international expansion further complicate the legal landscape. As AI facilitates seamless cross-channel operations and global reach, retailers must navigate a patchwork of international laws pertaining to trade, taxation, and digital services. Compliance becomes multifaceted, requiring a well-rounded legal strategy that encompasses local and international laws, ensuring that AI-enhanced operations don't inadvertently breach foreign regulations.

The legal challenges associated with AI in retail also encompass the responsibility of AI governance and accountability. Establishing clear guidelines for liability, transparency, and ethical AI usage is becoming increasingly crucial. Retail companies must consider establishing AI governance frameworks that encapsulate ethical considerations while defining accountability. When an AI system fails or causes harm, who is held responsible? Crafting these policies not only steers clear of legal entanglements but also contributes to building more robust and trustworthy AI systems.

Keeping abreast of all these legal aspects is no small feat, and the pace of technological advancement in AI means that some areas remain uncharted territory. There's an urgent need for cohesive and adaptable regulatory frameworks that incorporate expert insights while allowing room for innovation. Retailers find themselves at the intersection of technology and law, where proactive legal strategies are vital to successfully harnessing AI's potential while minimizing risks.

In conclusion, while the integration of AI into retail offers unprecedented opportunities for growth and efficiency, it simultaneously presents complex legal challenges that demand strategic foresight. Navigating these challenges requires a partnership between legal experts, technologists, and policymakers who can collectively shape a future where AI continues to innovate within the bounds of evolving legal landscapes. As AI becomes more pervasive in retail, the commitment to understanding and addressing these legal considerations will be a defining factor in determining which businesses thrive in this new era of commerce.

Formulating AI Governance in Retail

The rapid adoption of artificial intelligence (AI) in retail presents a unique set of challenges and opportunities for governance. As AI technology becomes increasingly embedded in the fabric of retail operations, there's a pressing need to establish comprehensive frameworks that define both the ethical deployment and the regulatory boundaries of AI systems. This section explores how these frameworks can be formulated, ensuring a balance between innovation and responsibility.

AI governance in the retail sector is not just a subject of ethical discourse but a critical commercial imperative. Without robust governance, retailers risk alienating customers, facing legal disputes, and damaging their brand reputation. The primary aim is to craft guidelines that protect consumer rights, ensure data privacy, and promote transparency. Moreover, retailers need governance structures that are flexible enough to adapt to the rapidly evolving AI landscape.

At the heart of AI governance is customer trust. Consumers are increasingly aware of how their data is used, and they demand more control and transparency. In the retail context, this means establishing clear protocols for data handling and usage. Retailers must articulate their practices in simple terms, offering consumers detailed insights into how their personal information influences product recommendations, dynamic pricing, and targeted advertising. This transparency will foster deeper trust between businesses and their customers, strengthening consumer loyalty.

Retailers must also navigate the intricate legal landscape that accompanies AI technology, which involves understanding and adhering to regulations like GDPR in the EU and CCPA in California. These regulations set a high standard for data protection and privacy, and companies must ensure they comply not only to avoid penalties but to uphold ethical standards. By embedding these legal considerations into their AI strategies, retailers can more effectively mitigate risks associated with data breaches and unauthorized data use.

An effective AI governance framework involves more than just compliance; it requires a commitment to ethical AI principles. This commitment can manifest in various ways, such as minimizing algorithmic biases and ensuring fairness in AI decision-making processes. For example, AI-driven pricing strategies should avoid unfair biases that could arise from faulty data or discriminatory algorithms. Retailers must actively audit their algorithms to identify and rectify any discriminatory patterns.

Retailers are not alone in this endeavor. Industry partnerships and collaborations with government agencies, non-profit organizations, and technological bodies can be pivotal. By participating in industry consortia focused on AI ethics, brands can align their governance frameworks with broader industry standards and contribute to a collective effort that shapes policy making and regulatory guidelines at large. This cooperative approach can help create a standardized framework that outlines clear expectations for AI use in retail.

Moreover, fostering an organizational culture that values ethics and transparency is key. Retailers could appoint dedicated AI ethics officers or committees responsible for overseeing AI projects. These individuals would be tasked with reviewing AI applications against established ethical guidelines, conducting regular audits, and ensuring continuous alignment with the latest regulations and technological advancements.

The role of AI governance extends beyond rules and regulations; it's also about shaping the future of AI in retail with deliberate innovation. Governance should encourage retailers to experiment with AI in ways that are creative yet cautious, innovative yet informed. Emphasizing a culture of open inquiry encourages teams to explore AI's full potential responsibly, driving forward-thinking solutions that enhance the customer experience while ethical considerations are thoughtfully weighed.

Ultimately, effective AI governance in retail aims to find equilibrium—balancing the immense potential of AI with the rights and concerns of the consumer. By fostering an environment of trust, transparency, and, most importantly, accountability, retailers can unleash AI's transformative power while safeguarding their most valuable asset: the customer relationship. This not only strengthens the retailer's position in an increasingly competitive market but also paves the way for sustainable growth and consumer advocacy.

Moving forward, as the AI ecosystem continues to mature, retailers will find themselves at the forefront of pioneering governance frameworks that not only adhere to regulatory requirements but also set new precedents for ethical AI use. In doing so, the retail industry has the opportunity to serve as a role model for other sectors, demonstrating that technological advances need not come at the cost of consumer rights and ethical standards. Through responsible governance, AI can indeed transform retail in ways that are both groundbreaking and principled.

Chapter 24:
Building an AI-Driven Retail Strategy

In an era where technology and consumer expectations are evolving at an unprecedented pace, crafting an AI-driven retail strategy is not just a competitive edge—it's a necessity. Retailers must navigate a landscape where AI influences every customer touchpoint, providing personalized experiences and operational efficiency. Building such a strategy involves more than just implementing AI tools; it requires a profound understanding of how these technologies can align with and elevate business goals. The key lies in integrating AI solutions that are not only innovative but also effective in creating tangible competitive advantages. By harnessing AI's capabilities, retailers can make proactive decisions, streamline processes, and anticipate consumer demands, ultimately leading to a more responsive and agile organization. Whether it's refining product recommendations or optimizing inventory, an AI-driven approach necessitates a balance of creativity and analytical thinking, transforming challenges into opportunities for growth and innovation in the retail sector.

Implementing AI Solutions Effectively

Successfully integrating AI into your retail strategy is akin to orchestrating a symphony where every piece plays a crucial part. It's not just about adopting cutting-edge technologies but about ensuring these tools are deployed in a way that enhances overall business objectives. Effectively implementing AI solutions requires a holistic approach, starting with a deep understanding of the organization's current capabilities and a clear vision of the desired outcomes. This process isn't instantaneous; it demands thoughtful planning and a strategic roadmap that aligns AI capabilities with retail business goals.

To begin with, crafting a compelling AI strategy involves identifying the specific pain points within your retail operations that AI can address. Whether it's optimizing inventory management, refining customer service, or enhancing supply chain operations, the first step is to pinpoint where AI can deliver the most significant impact. By focusing on these critical areas, retailers can prioritize their efforts and resources, ensuring maximum returns on their AI investments. This approach not only enhances operational efficiency but also contributes to a seamless customer experience, a fundamental requirement in today's digital era.

Once the problem areas have been identified, the next step is to build a data-driven culture within the organization. Data forms the backbone of any AI-driven solution, and building robust data management practices is crucial. This involves collecting quality data, ensuring its accuracy, and overcoming silos that could hinder data accessibility. Retailers must invest in the necessary infrastructure to support data collection and analytics, allowing for real-time insights and informed decision-making. Adopting cloud-based solutions can facilitate this by providing scalable storage and computing power without requiring heavy upfront investments.

It's equally important to foster a mindset among employees that embraces change and values data-driven insights. Regular training sessions and workshops can transform how staff interact with technology, enabling them to leverage AI effectively in their day-to-day operations. By cultivating a culture of continuous learning, team members are encouraged to remain curious and adaptable, skills which are invaluable as AI continues to evolve at a rapid pace.

Developing AI models that align with your business needs is the next vital step. This typically involves collaboration between data scientists, retail experts, and IT professionals to ensure the models are tailored to the specific nuances of the retail industry. It's essential to start with pilot projects, allowing teams to test and refine AI applications in a controlled environment. These projects serve as a proving ground, providing valuable insights and helping to mitigate risks before scaling solutions across the organization.

Moreover, integrating AI solutions effectively demands a keen awareness of emerging technologies and ample flexibility to incorporate them as they arise. Models need to be continually refined and updated to keep pace with changing trends and consumer behaviors. This iterative process of evaluation and adaptation is crucial for maintaining competitive advantage and enabling retail businesses to respond dynamically to market changes.

A significant factor in successful implementation is the choice of AI partners. Collaboration with technology providers and consultants who bring a wealth of expertise and experience is indispensable. These partnerships often provide access to a broad spectrum of resources, including advanced tools and platforms that might be too costly or complex for retailers to develop internally. By leveraging external knowledge and solutions, retailers can accelerate their AI journey without straining their in-house resources.

Ensuring effective implementation also means addressing the ethical considerations AI brings to the table. Consumers are increasingly aware of privacy issues and demand transparency in how their data is used. Retailers must navigate this by implementing robust governance frameworks that ensure compliance with data protection regulations and build trust with their customer base. Demonstrating a strong commitment to ethical AI practices not only safeguards the business from legal repercussions but can also serve as a differentiating factor in the marketplace.

Finally, measurable success criteria should be established to evaluate the effectiveness of AI solutions. These metrics need to align with broader business objectives and provide clear insights into how AI contributes to achieving these goals. From boosting sales conversion rates to reducing operational costs or improving customer satisfaction ratings, these KPIs offer tangible evidence of AI's impact, guiding strategic adjustments and ensuring continuous improvement.

As retailers venture into the realm of AI, maintaining an agile approach to implementation will be essential. The landscape is ever-changing, and what might work today may need adjustments tomorrow. Those who remain open to experimentation, willing to pivot strategies when necessary, and committed to leveraging AI's full potential are most likely to lead the future of retail. Implementing AI solutions effectively is not a destination but a journey, one that promises great rewards for those willing to innovate and explore the possibilities it offers.

Creating Competitive Advantages

In the ever-evolving landscape of retail, creating competitive advantages with AI goes beyond the adoption of technology—it's about leveraging innovation to transform challenges into opportunities. Retailers are no longer just implementing AI; they're strategically harnessing it to reshape their business models and redefine success. The ability to process massive volumes of data and derive actionable insights provides a critical edge, enabling retailers to outperform rivals in customer engagement, operational efficiency, and market agility.

A key way retailers can build these advantages is by leveraging AI to understand and predict consumer behavior with unprecedented accuracy. Traditional market research methods are being outpaced by AI-driven analytics that offer real-time insights into shifting preferences. By tapping into vast datasets—ranging from social media trends to purchase histories—retailers can anticipate desires before they materialize. This foresight allows businesses to tailor their offerings more precisely, ensuring that they meet customers exactly where their needs are. Such responsiveness builds brand loyalty and enhances customer lifetime value.

Moreover, AI empowers retailers to differentiate themselves through hyper-personalization. By integrating machine learning algorithms that analyze individual shopping habits and preferences, businesses can provide unique, customized experiences at scale. This goes beyond mere product suggestions; it includes personalized marketing messages, tailored promotions, and even dynamic in-store experiences. Retailers who excel in this area can create a strong emotional connection with their customers, which not only increases satisfaction but also encourages repeat business, broadening the customer base over time.

Operationally, AI-driven insights streamline processes and optimize efficiencies, which is crucial for maintaining a competitive stance. Inventory management, for instance, becomes a sophisticated endeavor where AI predicts demand and optimizes stock levels, reducing wastage and ensuring availability. These optimizations lead to cost savings, enabling retailers to allocate resources more effectively— be it through reducing holding costs or optimizing human resource deployment in stores. When resources are used efficiently, companies can offer competitive pricing, improving their market position.

Another pivotal aspect is the enhancement of supply chain operations. AI's predictive analytics revolutionize logistics, enabling retailers to anticipate disruptions and adapt more swiftly. By fostering a responsive supply chain, companies can ensure quicker delivery times and enhance customer satisfaction. This logistical edge can be a decisive factor in retail success, particularly in an era characterized by instant gratification and next-day delivery expectations. Furthermore, a resilient supply chain minimizes the impact of external shocks, such as economic downturns or natural disasters, supporting sustained competitive advantage.

AI's role in pricing strategies also cannot be overstated. Competitive pricing is more than just a race to the bottom; it's about understanding market dynamics and optimizing pricing across various touchpoints. AI enables retailers to analyze competitor pricing, understand consumer price sensitivity, and adjust prices in real-time. Such agility allows retailers to maintain profitability while still appealing to cost-conscious consumers. Retailers utilizing AI-driven pricing strategies enjoy the dual advantage of maximized profit margins and enhanced value perception among customers.

Store environments too are becoming smarter, creating immersive experiences that appeal to tech-savvy shoppers. Through AI, retailers can enhance the physical shopping journey with real-time data insights that customize in-store interactions. From AI-powered kiosks to sensor-driven product recommendations, the experience is tailored at every touchpoint. A memorable in-store experience not only draws customers in but also encourages higher spend per visit, driving up overall sales performance.

Furthermore, AI enables retailers to automate and enhance marketing efforts, creating precision-targeted campaigns that yield better returns. By analyzing customer data, AI can segment audiences more effectively and tailor communications to fit specific interests and behaviors. This kind of targeted approach reduces marketing expenditure while increasing conversion rates, delivering a strong competitive advantage. Cutting through the noise and reaching consumers with relevant messages solidifies brand positioning in a saturated market.

Such advancements in creating competitive advantages aren't only relevant in single-channel approaches. The approach spills into the omnichannel strategies, where AI plays a central role in blending online and offline experiences seamlessly. Retailers can use data to create coherent and compelling customer journeys that transcend individual sales channels. Ensuring that customers have a consistent and personalized experience—regardless of whether they're engaging with the brand in-store, online, or through mobile devices—fortifies customer relationships and sets the retailer apart from the competition.

Ultimately, these competitive advantages are about seizing AI's potential to not only meet current consumer demands but also anticipate future trends. Retailers need to adopt a forward-thinking mindset, investing in AI capabilities that align with their strategic goals. It's the retailers who are willing to innovate and adapt that will carve out significant and sustainable competitive advantages in the AI-driven retail era. Embracing continual learning and adaptation ensures that retailers are not just keeping up with change but driving it. In this rapidly advancing field, the competitive landscape doesn't just reward those who react to changes, but those who proactively shape the market's future.

Chapter 25:
Case Studies in AI-Powered Retail

In the rapidly evolving landscape of retail, AI stands out as a transformative force, and there's no better way to understand this impact than through real-world case studies. Picture a leading global department store chain that implemented AI-driven visual recognition technology, enabling customers to effortlessly find and purchase clothing items by simply snapping a picture of a desired style on their smartphone. This innovation not only streamlined the shopping experience but also significantly increased online engagement and sales. At another retail giant, AI was employed to optimize supply chain logistics, resulting in a marked reduction in delivery times and operational costs. These examples, among others, highlight how pioneering retailers successfully integrate AI to drive consumer satisfaction and operational efficiency. Companies that embrace these technologies are not only enhancing their competitive edge but also reshaping the retail experience as we know it, providing valuable lessons for others aiming to harness the potential of AI in the dynamic world of commerce.

Successful AI Integration Stories

In the rapidly evolving retail landscape, some companies have not only embraced AI technologies but have seamlessly woven them into the fabric of their operations, creating success stories that continue to inspire the industry. These stories serve as exemplars, showcasing the transformative power of AI when thoughtfully integrated into retail strategies. By understanding their approaches, other retailers can glean insights on leveraging AI to drive growth, enhance customer experiences, and maintain competitiveness. Here, we explore some of these standout cases that highlight successful AI integration in retail.

One of the most compelling stories comes from an established global fashion retailer that revolutionized its inventory management through AI. Faced with perennial challenges of overstocking and stockouts, this company leveraged AI-driven demand forecasting. The system utilized vast datasets, including historic sales figures, market trends, and even weather forecasts, to predict customer demand with unprecedented accuracy. As a result, not only did the retailer optimize its inventory levels, but it also significantly reduced waste and improved overall customer satisfaction by ensuring that popular items were always available.

Another exemplary case is a major e-commerce platform that harnessed AI to transform its customer service operations. By deploying AI-powered chatbots, the company enhanced its ability to provide timely and effective customer support. The chatbots, which were equipped with natural language processing capabilities, could handle a wide variety of customer queries, from order tracking to product recommendations. This not only lightened the load on human customer service agents but also led to faster resolution of customer concerns, enhancing the consumer experience dramatically.

Furthermore, a leading grocery chain illustrates the power of AI in supply chain optimization. By integrating predictive analytics into its logistics operations, the company was able to streamline the flow of goods from suppliers to stores. AI solutions provided insights into optimal delivery routes, times, and transportation modes, considering factors like traffic patterns and delivery windows. This significant improvement in efficiency resulted in cost savings and fresher products on the shelves, thereby boosting both profitability and customer satisfaction.

In the realm of personalized shopping experiences, a well-known department store chain utilized AI to offer hyper-personalized recommendations to its users. By analyzing customer data and shopping behavior, the AI platform provided tailored product suggestions, creating a more engaging and relevant shopping journey. Customers appreciated the highly personalized service, likening it to having a personal shopping assistant, which greatly enhanced their loyalty and repeat purchases.

AI's potential extends to dynamic pricing strategies, as demonstrated by an online electronics retailer that implemented AI solutions to refine its pricing tactics. The AI tools continuously analyzed market data, competitor prices, and consumer demand fluctuations to adjust prices in real-time. This proactive strategy allowed the retailer to remain competitive while maximizing profits, adapting instantly to market conditions that would typically require manual adjustments.

Smart stores, a concept brought to life by a prominent global retailer, utilized AI and IoT technologies to bridge the gap between digital and in-store experiences. In these stores, customers experienced innovative features like AI-driven product recommendations on digital screens and seamless checkout options using computer vision technology. These advancements not only enhanced the shopping experience but also provided the retailer with valuable insights into customer preferences and behaviors, enabling further refinement of their offerings.

Additionally, the application of AI in visual search and product discovery has set apart certain retailers by making the shopping process more intuitive. A fashion e-tailer integrated AI-powered visual search tools that allowed customers to upload images to find similar items on the platform. This not only simplified product discovery for users but also highlighted the retailer's commitment to innovation, setting it apart in a crowded online marketplace.

Virtual and augmented reality have also been successfully integrated by retailers aiming to innovate the online shopping experience. A furniture giant developed an AR app that lets customers visualize how products look in their homes before purchase. This practical use of AI not only improved customer satisfaction by removing uncertainty from the buying decision but also boosted sales by enabling a more engaging and interactive experience.

Sustainability, a critical issue today, is another area where AI integration has proven successful. A prominent apparel company leveraged AI to optimize resource utilization and reduce waste in its production processes. The AI systems analyzed every step of the production line, identifying inefficiencies and suggesting improvements. This allowed the company to reduce its carbon footprint while saving costs, aligning economic benefits with environmental responsibility.

Retail analytics and insights have always been cornerstones of business strategy, and AI has amplified these capabilities exponentially. A leadership-focused retail chain used AI to mine big data, extracting valuable insights on customer trends and preferences. These insights were then used to tailor marketing campaigns, refine product lines, and enhance store layouts. AI's superior analytical capabilities allowed the retailer to make data-driven decisions swiftly, outperforming competitors relying solely on traditional methods.

Ultimately, these stories of successful AI integration illustrate a common theme: the commitment to embrace change and innovate continuously. Retailers driving such success have not only implemented AI to solve existing problems but have also reimagined their future strategies around these technologies. Their stories inspire a vision of retail that's not only efficient but also engaging, personalized, and responsive to the evolving needs of the consumer. These pioneering companies demonstrate that the path to becoming a leader in AI-powered retail is paved with strategic foresight, technological investment, and a relentless drive to deliver excellence.

It's clear from these cases that AI is not a mere tool but a transformative force reshaping retail. By learning from these successful integrations, other businesses can unlock AI's potential, harnessing its capabilities to innovate, thrive, and ultimately succeed in the competitive world of retail. These stories stand as testaments to the profound and lasting impact that AI can have when integrated thoughtfully and purposefully.

Lessons from Leading Retailers

In examining how artificial intelligence is revolutionizing the retail landscape, it's crucial to delve into the real-world applications demonstrated by industry frontrunners. These pioneers have not only embraced AI technologies with open arms but have also strategically integrated them into their operations to enhance customer satisfaction and drive business growth. The lessons that emerge from their journeys are invaluable for any retail professional looking to leverage AI effectively.

Leading retailers have recognized the power of AI in creating hyper-personalized shopping experiences. Companies like Amazon have implemented sophisticated recommendation algorithms that analyze vast amounts of customer data to predict purchasing behavior and suggest relevant products. This level of personalization has significantly boosted customer loyalty and sales, as shoppers feel more understood and valued. Retailers can learn from this by developing and fine-tuning their recommendation systems to cater to their unique customer base.

Moreover, optimizing inventory management is another critical lesson from these trailblazers. By harnessing AI-powered predictive analytics, retailers like Walmart have transformed their supply chain processes. They employ machine learning models to forecast demand with high accuracy, ensuring that inventory levels align perfectly with consumer needs. This minimizes overstock and stockout scenarios, effectively balancing cost and availability. Retailers can emulate this approach by investing in predictive tools that integrate seamlessly into existing systems.

AI's role in streamlining customer service cannot be overlooked. Retailers such as Sephora have revolutionized customer interactions with AI-driven chatbots and virtual assistants, enabling 24/7 support and freeing up human resources for more complex inquiries. These virtual agents rapidly resolve common issues and provide personalized advice, fostering a more engaging and satisfying customer experience. Businesses that adopt similar AI tools can enhance their service offerings while reducing operational costs.

Dynamic pricing is another domain where AI has shown tremendous impact. Retail giants like Zara utilize AI algorithms to adjust prices in real-time based on factors such as demand, competition, and market trends. This helps maintain competitive pricing and maximizes profitability without alienating price-sensitive customers. Retailers seeking to implement such strategies should consider deploying AI-driven pricing models that are responsive and aligned with their financial objectives.

AI has also propelled smart store concepts by blending traditional shopping with digital innovations. Brands like Nike have launched technologically enhanced retail spaces equipped with IoT devices and AR experiences, offering customers a unique shopping journey that seamlessly integrates the physical and digital. These cutting-edge stores not only attract customers but also provide valuable data on shopping behaviors. Retailers can take inspiration from these smart stores to redefine their physical spaces and create memorable customer experiences.

Meanwhile, enhancing marketing through AI is another lesson that cannot be underestimated. Targeted AI-driven marketing campaigns, employed by companies like Target, better understand customer segments and tailor promotions to individual preferences. This increases the relevance and effectiveness of marketing efforts, ultimately driving higher conversion rates. To mirror this success, retailers should enhance their data analytics capabilities to uncover actionable customer insights.

The application of AI in e-commerce is another area where leading retailers have set benchmarks. Platforms powered by AI, such as those used by Alibaba, streamline online shopping experiences by personalizing product recommendations and optimizing search functionalities. This ensures that customers quickly find what they're looking for, reducing friction during purchases. It's imperative for other retailers to invest in robust AI-driven e-commerce platforms that cater to evolving consumer expectations.

Lastly, the importance of AI-driven workforce transformation should not be overlooked. Retailers like H&M are adopting AI to redefine retail roles, emphasizing the need for skills in data analysis and technology management. As AI automates repetitive tasks, the focus shifts towards strategic decision-making and human interaction. Retailers must embrace this shift by upskilling their workforce and fostering a culture that supports innovation and adaptation.

In conclusion, the lessons gleaned from leading retailers highlight several core themes: personalization, efficiency, responsiveness, and innovation. By observing how these companies have successfully integrated AI into their business models, other retailers can draw inspiration and practical insights. The journey of AI integration is ongoing, and staying attuned to these lessons will be crucial as the retail industry continues to evolve.

Conclusion

The transformative wave of AI in the retail industry is not just a fleeting trend—it's a fundamental shift that's redefining the landscape of commerce. We've traversed through various facets of this evolution throughout this book, from personalized shopping and dynamic pricing to AI-driven payment solutions and virtual realities enhancing consumer interactions. These technologies are not merely supplementary. They're paving a new path for how retailers operate and connect with their customers.

One of the cornerstone impacts of AI is its ability to revolutionize consumer experiences. Personalized shopping experiences powered by data-driven insights have flipped the traditional model on its head. No longer are consumers faceless entities; they're dynamic individuals with distinct preferences, and AI ensures these preferences guide every interaction. This level of customization not only elevates satisfaction but also strengthens brand loyalty, creating a virtuous cycle of engagement and loyalty.

AI has also unshackled supply chain and inventory management from the rigidity of outdated methods. Through real-time monitoring and predictive analytics, retailers can now anticipate demand and manage stock with unprecedented accuracy. This agility not only reduces waste but also enhances sustainability efforts—a necessary step in today's environmentally-conscious market. It's an ecosystem where efficiency and responsibility are no longer mutually exclusive.

A significant area where AI has left an indelible mark is in customer service. Intelligent chatbots and automated systems have revolutionized the speed and quality of service, offering instantaneous support that meets the escalating expectations of modern consumers. While machines handle routine inquiries and processes, human employees are freed to tackle more complex issues, fostering innovation and personalized human interactions.

Security remains a paramount concern as we navigate through this AI-infused retail landscape. AI-driven payment solutions and fraud prevention mechanisms are essential not just for safeguarding transactions but for building a foundation of trust. As consumers become increasingly aware and concerned about data privacy, the onus is on retailers to deploy AI responsibly, ensuring that customer data is protected and used ethically.

As we stand on the cusp of future innovations, it's clear that the blend of AI and retail is still very much in its infancy. Emerging technologies promise to push these boundaries even further—ushering in advanced forms of artificial intelligence that could do more than respond to trends; they could start predicting them with a precision that was once unimaginable. From augmented reality fittings to smart stores equipped with IoT technology, the possibilities are as exciting as they are endless.

This journey doesn't come without its challenges. Technical barriers, ethical dilemmas, and consumer trust issues continue to pose significant hurdles. Retailers embarking on this AI journey must approach these challenges with agility, adaptability, and a commitment to ethical practices. Developing a sound governance framework will be crucial in ensuring that AI-driven innovations align not just with business goals but with societal values and legal standards.

AI has the potential to democratize access to quality retail experiences, breaking down regional barriers and fostering inclusivity.

This opportunity, however, demands a recognition of regional diversity and a tailored approach that respects cultural nuances and market peculiarities. The future of AI in retail is a global conversation, one that requires collaboration and knowledge-sharing across borders.

In conclusion, the journey of integrating AI into retail is undoubtedly complex but loaded with possibilities. The key lies in a balanced approach that embraces innovation while respecting traditional retail values. Entrepreneurship spirit, coupled with a keen sense of technological curiosity, will be vital as retail leaders and innovators embark on this path. While the specifics of future advancements are yet to unfold, one thing is clear: AI is here to stay, and its potential to revolutionize retail is just beginning to be tapped.

Embracing the revolution requires forward-looking strategies, an openness to change, and the courage to leap into the unknown. The retail industry, as we once knew it, is transforming into a vibrant, intelligent ecosystem—an exciting frontier where technology and human creativity coexist to create unparallel shopping experiences. As we close this exploration into AI's impact on retail, we must acknowledge that this is not an end but a beginning, a new chapter that invites continuous learning, adaptability, and a relentless quest for excellence.

Appendix A:
Resources for Further Reading

As artificial intelligence continues to shape the retail landscape, staying informed is crucial for anyone looking to navigate this rapidly evolving field. Below is a curated list of resources that provide deeper insights into the topics discussed throughout this book. These works offer varying perspectives from academics, industry experts, and business leaders, each contributing valuable knowledge to help you further understand AI's transformational impact on retail.

Books and Publications

"Artificial Intelligence for Retail: A Practical Guide" by Francien Nel: This book covers the fundamental concepts of AI applications in retail, offering practical examples and case studies that highlight successful AI strategies in the industry.

"The Fourth Industrial Revolution" by Klaus Schwab: Explore the broader context of technological evolution, including AI, and how it impacts various industries, including retail. Schwab provides insights into the global impact of these technologies.

"Predictive Analytics: The Power to Predict Who Will Click, Buy, Lie, or Die" by Eric Siegel: Gain an understanding of predictive analytics, a core component of AI, and its application in forecasting consumer behavior and optimizing retail operations.

Academic Journals and Articles

Journal of Retailing: Regularly featuring peer-reviewed articles, this journal covers cutting-edge research on retail operations, consumer behavior, and emerging technologies in the retail sector.

MIT Sloan Management Review: Look for articles that explore the adoption of AI in business strategies, focusing on technological adaptation, leadership, and innovation in retail.

Online Platforms and Courses

edX: "Artificial Intelligence: Business Strategies and Applications": This course offers a comprehensive overview of AI, focusing on practical strategies for implementing AI solutions in business environments.

Coursera: "AI for Everyone" by Andrew Ng: A beginner-friendly course that demystifies AI, providing essential knowledge for those interested in incorporating AI technologies into their retail strategies.

Industry Reports and Whitepapers

McKinsey & Company: "The State of AI in 2023": Examine the current trends, challenges, and opportunities for AI implementation across different sectors, with insights applicable to retail.

Deloitte: "AI is Changing the Face of Retail": This whitepaper delves into how AI is revolutionizing retail operations, enhancing customer interactions, and offering a competitive edge for businesses.

Websites and Blogs

Wired - Retail: Stay updated with the latest news and trends in technology and retail, exploring how advancements like AI are transforming the industry.

Retail Dive: A valuable source for industry news, covering everything from emerging tech to consumer trends and regulatory changes impacting retail.

Diving into these additional resources will provide you with a richer understanding of AI's multifaceted role in reshaping modern retail. Whether you're an industry veteran or a newcomer eager to explore, these materials serve as a strong foundation for building your knowledge and inspiring innovation in your own endeavors.

www.ingramcontent.com/pod-product-compliance
Lightning Source LLC
Chambersburg PA
CBHW051239050326
40689CB00007B/990